Rites of Passage

Rites of Passage

✦

My Schizophrenic Youth in Mosaic

Jason Stuart Ratcliff

Writers Club Press
San Jose New York Lincoln Shanghai

Rites of Passage
My Schizophrenic Youth in Mosaic

Writers Club Press
an imprint of iUniverse, Inc.

For information address:
iUniverse, Inc.
5220 S. 16th St., Suite 200
Lincoln, NE 68512
www.iuniverse.com

ISBN: 0-595-23846-7

Printed in the United States of America

When the unclean spirit has gone out of a person, it wanders through waterless regions looking for a resting place, but not finding any, it says, "I will return to my house from which I came." When it comes, it finds it swept and put in order. Then it goes and brings seven other spirits more evil than itself, and they enter and live there; and the last state of that person is worse than the first.

—Luke 11:24-26

1

I see it—I am the only one who sees it, and there is an awful desire in me to tell the world of it. It is the city, but it is not an ordinary thing I see. Everyone's movements, everyone's every expenditure of energy is prescribed. The cars all move in predictable patterns and formulas—I can predict when they will stop, when they will slow, when they will speed up—I know which ones are about to turn and what way. They move through the city like blood cells, carrying themselves along as if they are only parts in some vast organism that I am inside, that I too am a part of. I cannot see the limits of this organism; everything I see has arisen out of it, and exists only by virtue of its systemic functioning. All the buildings, all the stores, the landscaping, the streets signs and stoplights—they are all It. I am not its enemy, I am not here to tear it down, I am not a revolutionary or an extremist. I am here to tell the world that It exists—no one can make a single movement but that the movement is an expression of it, and yet no one sees it but me, no one even knows it exists. I am here to tell the world of It.

I'm sure these ideas sound psychotic. That's because they are. I look at things this way because I'm schizophrenic. Let me explain.

Psychosis is a break from reality. Any fool can tell you that. And schizophrenia is a disease of psychosis. What does this mean? That my brain won't work? That I have disordered thought? Let me ask you something. If reality were completely objective, if there were nothing that existed that weren't reality, how would one break from it? Wouldn't one be as stuck inside it, merely by virtue of living in it, as a stone is stuck with being a stone? A healthy mind—your mind—must process reality, must find out what to emphasize and what to push into the background, must draw connections between experiences in a meaningful way. This is how reality comes about. It is constructed by your mind—a healthy mind. My mind cannot construct it like yours does. Am I getting psychotic again? I cannot quite tell.

When I take classes at the university—and I have decided only tonight never to take one again—I write philosophical papers. I'm a philosophy major. I write very rationally, and get As in all my classes (at the university I transferred to in 1999, I have only one A-). Unless the professors can tell from my slovenly dress and shyness with other students, they have no idea I'm schizophrenic. I always thought, based on my performance in these classes, that I could spot psychotic ideas when I write them down, and can see what logically follows from what—the rules of logic are like arithmetic, very clear. Except. I recently wrote a 140-page essay on schizophrenic belief systems in the context of ideas coming from Existentialism and cultural anthropology. I won't bore you with the details. I was going to publish. I was going to be hailed as an intellectual figure, a man of analytic genius. My essay explained many unresolved issues in science, even ones having nothing to do with schizophrenia. In a one-paragraph digression, I showed in the clearest way a simple logical invalidity in the Ontological Argument for the existence of God, which no one had seen before. But then it hit me. Perhaps my essay explained too much. It even, after all, explained the biological purpose of the phenomenon of dreams. Yes, then it hit me.

2

I usually write in the morning. Except lately. Lately I've been writing all day. Some psychiatrists consider compulsive writing a psychotic symptom. It probably is.

The problem is this: I view my creative writing as art. Hence my desire to actually get my novels published. How many have I written? More than I want to admit. They all sit on my computer waiting for me to go through and edit them, and once I am done they go back into that sad oblivion of the unread novel. It doesn't, ultimately, matter if I get them published. But focusing on fantasies of the future—future appreciation of my art—has an important function in my present mental health. Without such fantasies about the future—and it doesn't matter in the least if that future comes true—I would be left to fantasize psychotically about much worse things. I have found over the years that I need at least some level of a delusion; if I go very long with none, a new one will develop. I have, over the past few years, quite neatly avoided this. I write, I hope to get published, I am an under-appreciated artist who will one day get recognition—this is sane enough. With this idea to occupy my mind, I am able to live a little more normally.

But is it true?

3

When I was in my first psychological hospital—I was just 17—I remember very clearly my first physical takedown. But let me start from the beginning. You see, even when psychotic in the months before I was admitted, I had found immense pleasure in music. It was, really, my only pleasure. I would walk home from the place where the school bus dropped me off, alone, wondering what to do when I got home. I won't get into the psychotic delusion I was under until later. But I would say to myself on my way home, "What to do when I get home? Take a piss? And then what? Listen to music. Yes, listen to music." And so I would go home, take a piss, and then listen to music. It was all I wanted, besides the bong hits I took from a bong that was in the form of a ceramic skull.

Anyway, that was one of the things I missed in the hospital, my music. One day, I looked into the nurse's station, and saw that my father had dropped off my stereo. I was very excited. I immediately asked for it. I was refused. I demanded it. I was still refused. I was still psychotic. I had refused any medication, and my therapist had decided not to force it on me. I was told they were afraid I would break my records and use them to slash my wrists. The idea hadn't even occurred to me. They had figured out my plans before I myself had formed them.

To make a long story short, when I was told to walk into the day-room, sit down, and stop asking for my stereo, it was my turn to refuse. The next thing I knew hands were grabbing at me from all sides, I was on the floor and someone was lying across my back, my limbs were being folded up so they could lift me onto the gurney. Soon, I found myself locked in seclusion. It didn't have padded walls, like in the movies. It had cinderblock walls. I don't know why it didn't have pad-ded walls. If someone banged his head into the walls until he died, whose fault would it be? It wouldn't be theirs—they didn't tell him to do it. I didn't bang my head into the walls. I screamed. I went on screaming for hours, until I was exhausted.

At dinnertime, someone came to the door, and told me to sit in the corner, with my face to the wall. I did so. He came in and carefully set a tray of food by the door. There was another door right next to him—the bathroom door. There was a bathroom and shower in this seclusion room—of course we weren't animals. I said to him, as he set down the tray, "I haven't been physically out of control at all." I had merely refused direction, after all, and had only reacted after they had grabbed a hold of me. Somehow I expected him to react to my state-ment; I expected that he would give their side of the controversy, that he would explain to me what, in their eyes, I had done wrong. I more than expected this—I was certain it would come. It seemed perfectly natural that such a discussion would take place. Most people, after all, when given a statement they blatantly disagree with, will engage the person in discussion. It is only natural.

But he only said to me, "Okay," backed out the door, and locked it shut.

4

I didn't mention it when I saw him later. By the next day, after having masturbated in the shower, I was much too concerned about other things. I was concerned, in particular, about the rest of the patients all getting together behind my back, and talking about the unusual number of times I had masturbated in the space of only one week (twice).

5

There is a word, a particularly powerful word, that is just now coming to mind. "Sick." What does this word mean? It implies some sort of illness. But when I was in high school, things like deviant sex acts were "sick"; things like bizarre, obscene behavior was "sick"; anything that utterly revolted, that made one despise, that was something to be completely shunned, was "sick". That was in high school. That was before I became sick. That was when I went along with the rest of them, went along agreeing that certain things were sick, looking down upon everyone who was perverted enough to actually be sick. Homosexuals were sick. Perverts were sick. That was before I became sick.

Much of what you read here will be sick. It will be hard to relate to. Don't be surprised if you say to yourself, "This guy is sick." Schizophrenia, though perhaps the most tragic of diseases, is not a triumph-over-tragedy tale you see on daytime talk. And not because we don't sometimes triumph. Because, when we start to tell our tales, to tell of the distortion and ugliness in our very minds and hearts, people do not say so much, "That must be terrible for you," but rather, "It must be terrible to be you."

One time, not long ago, I was commenting on the frightening appearance of a doll my step-niece particularly liked. My stepsister, her mother, agreed that it was frightening. I said, "It's like one of those dolls in the movies that come alive and chop people up." "Yeah," said my stepsister, "you mean like some sort of psycho baby."

6

There are two things schizophrenics usually have some neurosis about: religion, and sex. I'll probably get around to neurosis about sex eventually. However: religion.

I used to be quite religious. This was when I lived in an apartment in Los Angeles with two others. Imagine three men living together, each of whom has one mental illness or another, none of whom is very motivated to clean up after himself, or clean up after anyone else. Furthermore, imagine that this is in West Los Angeles, a few miles inland from Venice Beach, where cockroaches even infest the streets, and are seen usually at sunset coming out of the storm drains and scrambling about. Imagine this, and you may get some notion of how many cockroaches we had in our apartment. I used to open the cabinets in the kitchen above my head, and they would be running in circles all about the inside of the door, some of them falling onto my shoulder. I was used to it, though. I had lived like this for years. But I digress.

In those days, I was determined to live up to Jesus's commands such as are found in the Sermon on the Mount. I went to a small Seventh-Day Adventist congregation every Saturday, and prayed passionately, unloading everything in my heart, every morning and evening. Whenever I thought of treating myself to a candy bar, I said to myself, "That 65 cents could go to the homeless," and if I ever gave in and bought one, I felt guilty, as if I had cheated the homeless. If an acquaintance were in particular distress, I would fast for 48 hours, taking only water, to pray for the person. The more I lived like this, the more I was sure I would be canonized as a saint one day. The more I thought I would be canonized as a saint one day, the more I felt guilty for committing the sin of pride. You might say I was very...focused. Yes, I was very focused on my religion.

Anything that smacked of obscenity, anything that had to do with "dirty" lust, I avoided. I was aware enough to know that it would be unhealthy to quit masturbating (though I did try a couple of times), but if I looked at the underwear ads in the newspaper, I felt guilty. I hardly ever did. I imagined my ideal woman in these days. She was modestly dressed, never said a curse word, had nothing impure in her heart. One day, I was in the Santa Monica College library, and I noticed a young nun in a habit sitting at one table. I found myself wanting to start a conversation with her; I was very drawn to her. I sat across from her. I made eyes at her. I thought of starting a conversation, but something told me it would be terribly inappropriate. I realized suddenly that she was a nun, after all, and left.

Where was I going with this? Oh yes: religion. This is a picture of my most stable, longest lasting experience with a particular religion. It didn't make me happy. Gradually, I grew bitter toward it. That was before I converted to Islam. Which was before I left Islam and began taking classes at a Catholic church in order to prepare for my baptism (I have never been baptized). Which was before I grew nervous about getting baptized and quit the classes, and went back to Islam. Which was before I left Islam again. Now, I will try with a feeble effort to make all the five daily prayers and drink no alcohol for a few months, and then give up and leave Islam again, only to return later. A Muslim would say I need more faith. I think I need less. I am glad I'm only going through the motions with religion now. I know what it's like to have strong faith. It made me so unhappy that I have become somewhat bitter.

My paintings are mostly Expressionist pictures of anguish with crosses here and there. There is one I am looking at right now (it is on the wall I face when at my computer). It is a crucifixion scene, with a solid black circle over Jesus's face, and concentric black circles surrounding it, going out in waves to the edges of the paper. The last time my sister was at my apartment, she commented on the paintings. "I would think someone like you would think it's blasphemous to put crosses in those paintings," she said. She knows how devoted I used to be. "Those paintings make it look like you're bitter toward religion." "I probably am," I said.

7

I mentioned earlier that I have been writing all day lately. Before starting the present work, I was working on my 140-page theory of schizophrenia. I have been writing all day lately, unable to stop the ideas from coming, because I recently made a change in my medication. With no medication, there would be no way to stop writing. You see, the psychotic mind is constantly thinking in a logical progression. If P then Q. If Q then R. There is nothing illogical in the steps taken. It's just that P itself is something purely imagined. Thus are psychotic delusions built. It helps ease psychosis to write the ideas down. Thus, the origin of my creative writing projects. I wonder if it would inspire jealousy, or pity, in a normie writer who has writer's block, if I told him all I would have to do is stop taking my pills, and I would not be able to contain the ideas that would come.

8

Here's the problem. Fiction is at its best when it is an honest expression of the particular view of the world of the author. What is my world? A psychotic world. Thus, over the past few years, I have been trying to express that word by writing psychotic rambling. Three quarters of a century after Joyce, one might think psychotic rambling would be something the literary art world might be open to. It is not. I query publishers explaining that I am schizophrenic, and when they read my novel samples, they say, "But this is only psychotic rambling." Actually, I do not know what they say. Perhaps they say something else; I have no idea. All I know is that, as far as my psychotic rambling goes, it is extremely interesting psychotic rambling. Difficult, but interesting. But I do believe that if someone does actually say, "This is only psychotic rambling" this is viewed as a genuine criticism. I do not know if it is a genuine criticism; I think many would say it is, and no one is really "right" or "wrong". I can't argue with such a criticism. If "This is only psychotic rambling" is a genuine criticism, my writing, merely by having been written by a psychotic as an honest expression of his world, is worthless. If psychotic rambling itself is worthless, how is a schizophrenic to keep his expression of his world from being worthless?

9

I sometimes wonder why psychosis in visual art is thought good, and psychosis in literary art is thought bad. I paint as well as write, but I don't paint very much. My painting is as psychotic as my writing, and it is quite conventional in the world of painting at large. So conventional, in fact, that it cannot be very important work. But when I bring my writing to a creative writing workshop at the university, I get reactions like, "This isn't fiction—there are no scenes or story," and, "This is just disjointed." Psychosis in literary art does not make for conventional art. I think part of the reason why the visual art world has become accepting of psychosis, is that painting itself is not a psychotic symptom. But writing is. Since so many schizophrenics write psychotic things, it is hard for the literary art world to accept and absorb it. When a schizophrenic is a painter, he is probably not a psychotic who paints as a psychotic symptom, but an artist who happens to be psychotic. When a schizophrenic is a writer, he is a writer because of psychosis. He need not actually have an artist's mindset or personality, on top of his psychosis. But what if a schizophrenic does have the mindset of an artist, is an artist on top of being psychotic, but happens to be a writer instead of a painter? I do not know what will happen to him, but I would not like to be him.

10

I am in the habit of drinking Turkish coffee. I get it at a little Middle-Eastern grocery by the Islamic Center in Aurora. It is coffee that is ground so fine, the coffee powder is put directly into the cup, and then boiling water is poured into the cup. The coffee powder all settles at the bottom. Once I drink it to the thick dregs at the bottom, I rinse out the cup in my sink. I don't wash all the wet coffee dregs down the drain. It builds up in my sink. Right now, there is more than a quarter-inch layer of what looks like mud on the bottom of my sink, underneath some dishes. Why don't I wash it down? It doesn't bother me. Normies will look at it, and it will cause a disturbance. It does not cause any disturbance in me. Neither does going a week without showering or brushing my teeth.

11

But why this obsession with getting published? Why not just write?

Once, in that apartment full of cockroaches I mentioned earlier, for about a month I was convinced I could send my thoughts to people on TV. And not only did the newscasters and talk show hosts know my thoughts, but everyone who was watching the shows knew them—it had to do with the airwaves, I don't remember precisely how it worked. I was, for that month, the talk of the whole nation. Pot smoking college students would gather around their TVs and watch as my thoughts made the voices of the newscasters waver, made them uncomfortable, made them struggle to keep to the script. Sometimes the newscasters commented on this fact—the fact of me and my thoughts, which of course everyone was aware of—sometimes they commented on it covertly, in a way that everyone understood, because everyone was on the same page. No one discussed this telepathic phenomenon on TV overtly, but they did so around the water cooler in offices and on TV news sets when the cameras were off. My very thoughts, and all my personality, were known intimately by the whole nation. I was famous, and my sense of solitude only grew. It wasn't merely because, as they say, "It's lonely at the top." It was because this world in which I was famous, which was the world I saw when I went down the street to the grocery or bus stop, was one of my own spontaneous invention, and I was its sole inhabitant. No one lived in this world but I, so that it became a world of utter solitude for me. And I didn't know it wasn't real; all I knew was that I could not interact with another human being so that our minds really met, and we understood each other. We lived, after all, in different worlds.

I still have this sense of solitude, and I have had it all my adult life. When I think of people reading this, and knowing me, and understanding me, I say to myself, "Ah, yes, now people understand me, now I am not so alone." But I know this will not really cure my sense of solitude; it only seems like it now. Perhaps the only reason I believed the newscasters could hear my thoughts, was because I desired to make myself known to people so much, to live in a world of true interaction, that my desire could no longer be contained anymore by what was real and true and possible.

12

When I was about 21 or 22, I flew from Los Angeles to El Paso, Texas, to meet my father, stepmother, and a friend of my father's, Paul. We were going on a trip into the state of Chihuahua, to a large canyon off in the mountains called, in English, Copper Canyon. I knew this canyon was inhabited by Tarahumara Indians, and didn't really know what to expect; somehow I expected them to be adept at hunting and sneaking up on people, and given to engaging in strange ceremonies around fires at night, beating drums and singing. Basically, I thought we ought to take care with them.

On the phone with my father before my flight, he reminded me, "Be sure you don't forget your medication. If you forget it, that's one of the few things that could make us have to cancel the trip." I took my medication, but only one of them. I decided all I would really need was my antipsychotic, Loxapine, not my antidepressant. But when I went to take my medication, I only looked at the capsules; I didn't look at the labels. They had only that month changed the look of my antidepressant, so that I took it for my antipsychotic. That was the only medication I brought, and I didn't even know it.

By the night of the day we entered Mexico at Juarez, I was in my own hotel room in the city of Chihuahua. I was certain someone was about to break in and try to murder me. I was terrified. What could I do? After all, this wasn't my country; it wasn't my turf, and I was at a disadvantage when it came to defending myself. They knew it, and "they" were ready to devour me—"they" hated me for being here; I was an intruder and I didn't belong here, and so they would murder me. I was the object of a hatred so intense it could accomplish every violence against me.

The more disturbed I got, the more of my antidepressant capsules I swallowed. I still thought it was my antipsychotic. I didn't understand why it hadn't made me sleepy yet. The more of them I swallowed, the more the patterns of my thought moved along with increasing complexity and imagination. I was ready to kill anyone who broke into my hotel room and threatened me—and certainly someone would at any minute. I lay undressed in bed with the light on staring at the peeling sky-blue paint on the door, waiting. But what if I killed someone who had tried to kill me? I would certainly go to Mexican prison for the rest of my life. Ah! There was no escaping "them", the ones whom I had intruded on, who hated me. If I killed them, my fate would be worse than if I let them kill me.

The next day I was a little calmer. I tried to hide the fact that I was so disturbed from the rest of my party. I was constantly on edge—looking for native Mexicans who could certainly try to kill me at any moment, but not wanting to jump the gun with anyone. We ate breakfast in a little restaurant. We refused the water they offered at the restaurant and drank from our water bottles. My father's friend Paul ordered a coffee at the restaurant, and though I too wanted coffee and was assured by him it wouldn't make me sick, I thought he was incredibly stupid to drink it, and told him so.

Ever since the trip had begun, Paul and I had been in a little of a competition on who could speak the best Spanish. I think he could speak it better than I; but both of us probably sounded ridiculous when we tried it, I especially. I had taken one semester of Spanish at Santa Monica College, in which class I had memorized maybe 200 words, and certain phrases and syntactical structures. But when I tried to actually communicate, in my disturbed state, a string of Spanish words would come out of my mouth, but I don't think they really made much sense. It might have made it sound like I spoke Spanish pretty well, to my father and stepmother, who didn't speak any; but whomever I was speaking to didn't seem to understand. I tried to use my Spanish at every opportunity, and thought I was doing very well with it. After all, the phrases in my mind made sense to me. I just don't think they made actual Spanish sense, made sense to anyone but me.

Digression is very natural to the psychotic frame of mind. And so I digress. Thoughts lead to thoughts lead to thoughts, until I have left my subject matter completely behind. Bear with me. I have a hard time really knowing what is "related" to my subject and what isn't. This is something most people process unconsciously; things "seem" related or unrelated. I have a hard time knowing when I digress, and so I digress. Have patience.

13

I spend a lot of time sitting and thinking. It's amazing how much time you can spend, with simple nicotine and caffeine addictions, doing nothing but thinking all day long. I do not work, and I am not signed up for any classes this semester. I hardly ever go out, even for a walk. I do not get bored. When my mother asks me what I have been doing with myself lately, I say, "Just reading and writing," but actually, I get very little reading done. I sit and think, and write down my thoughts. But back to my story.

We took the train from the city of Chihuahua out into the mountains toward Copper Canyon. At each of the stops, vendors would bring their wares onto the train and try to sell them to the passengers for as long as the train was stopped. I began to take an interest at all the folk art they were selling—multi-colored articles of clothing, different sorts of figurines and trinkets they had made by hand. They appeared alien to me, but not exactly threatening; only interesting. I didn't buy any of them, however. At one stop, when I went to the door to await the vendors, none came onto the train. I said to the Mexicans standing next to me, "No vendors?" They didn't understand. I had said this English question in my best Mexican accent. Somehow, I thought that "vendors" was a Spanish word, and I knew "no" was Spanish. I repeated my question when they said, "Eh?" again in my best Mexican accent. Finally they just said, "No." I don't know if they knew what I meant or not.

But these vendors' wares weren't the only things that seemed alien to me. Mexico itself seemed alien to me. It wasn't merely curious; it was frightening. All my perceptions were *Mexico,* wherever I looked, whomever or whatever I saw. There was no escaping it; I was *in* it, miles and miles into it. I still did not know I hadn't been taking my antipsychotic. I thought all this strangeness I was experiencing was the strangeness of Mexico; Mexico was frightening, bizarre, nothing made sense there, everything was threatening there. And I was going farther into it. My father and the rest of my party seemed unconcerned, seemed not to see the threat of Mexico; I merely thought they were naively going forth into dangers they had no concept of. If they were willing to go through with it, so was I. But it was my duty to keep their overconfidence and relaxation from exposing them to the dangers only I sensed; and I would only help them if I went along, since they did not see the dangerous place we really were in.

14

This is where I am now. I am in my studio apartment. I have been here all day. I have only gone out twice today, once to buy a turkey sandwich at 7-11, and the other time to buy a microwave burrito at the same store. It is somewhere between 10:00 and 10:30 at night. I have been listening to the radio all day. What particularly strikes me is the commercials. They seem to be saying, "Join in, join in, join in." They repeat this again and again hundreds of times a day to us, all of us. They are appealing to the mentality I was in during high school, the mentality that says, "Come, be one of the crowd; and then you too will be on the inside, like we are, and be able to despise everyone who is not one of the crowd." Everywhere I go people are buying things or using things they have bought—cars, cell phones, wireless internet. These commercials. They are making everyone join in, no one can help it, everyone is pushed along into being like everyone else. No one wants to be the last one left who has not joined in, everyone wants rather to be on the inside, and able to despise the last one left. The commercials *program* their minds. I have not joined in. I don't have the money. I do not envy the ones who have. I'm sure they do not envy me.

Am I getting psychotic again?

15

There are several small towns around the neighborhood of Copper Canyon. I do not remember the name of the one we got off the train at. I do remember the name of the small town we stayed two nights in before taking the train back. Creel. Since my visit, I have asked at least one Chihuaguense here in the US if he knew the town of Creel, who did. It is a very small town. He said it was named after a wealthy American who settled there long ago. I have no idea if what he said was true.

But we got off the train not at Creel, but an even smaller town whose name escapes me. By sunset, we were at a place from where it was easy to descend into the canyon. At least relatively easy; it didn't seem particularly easy anywhere. There was a man who lived in a house not far from where we were camped, who offered to guide us the next day. We turned him down. The next day, we would go looking for him to take him up on the offer, without ever finding him. That night, his children—two boys—hung around our camp and ate with us. I assumed they were starving and needed food. I kept offering them more until they finally went away. My father told me once they were gone that he was under the impression they had only been eating it to be polite. The next morning they were there again. I tried to ask them in Spanish if they thought I spoke good Spanish. I had been speaking it to them all along, thinking I was making perfect sense. They only laughed when I asked them this, as they did to everything I said.

The night before, Paul had lit a campfire. I thought it was a terrible idea—what if he started a forest fire? He seemed to think there was no concern. I remember the way the fire grew and grew, seemed constantly to become larger and more terrible. The fire was like an evil in my world of perception, something I desperately wanted to extinguish and eliminate. Its very image was a source of anguish for me. What if it spread? What if we could no longer control it? I was terrified of the consequences, and kept telling Paul to put it out. He seemed to enjoy it, and would have nothing to do with my nonsense.

16

About eight years ago, a gigantic cyst developed on the back of my neck. It grew and grew; I had no idea what it was. One day, I squeezed it as hard as I could. The copious pus that came out smelled horrible—it gave me such satisfaction to get it finally out of my body. It was gone—I had done it. Over the years, I have, on and off, thought I felt a bump there, and squeezed it as hard as I could. Nothing ever comes out. There is a bump there, but whatever it is it is hard and deep under the skin. It's not very pronounced, hardly even noticeable. But it bothers me. I think to myself, "There it is, deep in my skin—a pocket of that horrible smelling pus," and I squeeze it as hard as I can. Just a week ago, I ran a knife over my stove flame, rinsed it off to cool it, and tried to slice open the cyst. The only thing that came out was blood. It was one of those knives with teeth, and it was very dull; I had to saw back and forth for some time, all to no avail. My father happens to be in town right now so I showed him the next time I saw him. "That's not a good idea," he said of my trying to slice at it with a knife. "If you get an infection there, it's very close to your spine." He pushed on the cyst. "I don't feel a cyst there," he said. "It could be scar tissue." I know he is right; I suspected it was only scar tissue before I tried to cut it open. But it was driving me crazy. I can still imagine the stale, festering smell that pus had when I burst the cyst years ago. I say to myself, "If *that*, is still in my body, I have to get it out."

17

The day we entered the canyon, my terror of the Indians was completely overtaking my psychology.

Two ragged dogs followed along with us; they seemed to think they might get some food out of it, and they were right. My father told me not to waste food by giving them any; but once the dogs had twice found us water (which we pumped through a filter, and then put iodine in) he said they ought to be rewarded with some food. I told him that the dogs had only been following their instincts when they found us water, and if we give them food, we ought to do it because we feel sorry for them; not because of any decisions they made to help us, since dogs aren't capable of decisions. Anyway, we were in agreement that they should be given some food.

When we came to an empty Indian house with a caved roof, I was sure the Indians were watching us, were tracking us, were going to kill us if we offended them too deeply. I could see inside the Indian house through the caved roof, and saw some farming equipment, some dried corncobs, and bits and pieces of a life that was mysterious to me. The rest of my party began to take pictures and walk inside. I was horrified at the idea—didn't my father say these Indians didn't like having their pictures taken? Weren't we foolishly offending them by going inside, in their very home country, where they would have every advantage were they to decide to murder us? The rest of my party only talked about silly observations and things they knew—the Tarahumaras grew corn in the spring, and would occupy this house then; for now, they had moved to other parts of the canyon, in order to subsist on their goats and other means. I told them we were deeply offending the Tarahumaras, that we were invading their homes, and they were certain to murder us. My stepmother said, "Relax. They wouldn't want to kill us, and even if they wanted to, they probably couldn't, or would have a very hard time doing it." I thought this was nonsense. Who ever thought that Indians couldn't kill white men and women in Indian country, when they set their minds to do it? We were in terrible danger here, and my party didn't even realize it.

I kept thinking of all the plans I had for my future—I would become a writer, I would one day write my masterpiece, I had important things in my life to accomplish. I knew my writing at the time wasn't as good as it would be in the future. Now I was going to die, and miss out on all that, and for what? Just this silliness, the silliness of coming here, the silliness of my father and stepmother who didn't see the danger we were in. I was going to die because of silliness, like a soldier, who all his life prepares to die in glory, and then dies from an infected cat scratch.

The descent into this canyon was a long process. We would follow the trails along the narrow plateaus, until they showed us a way down the cliffs that separated the plateaus from the plateaus. When we got to the plateau we would camp at, this one was very narrow: on one side was a cliff that went up, and about twenty feet in the other direction, dropping off at varying degrees of sheerness, was a cliff that went down into the abyss. The plateau itself wasn't quite a plateau, but was angled slightly downward, so that the farther one went to the right (from the direction of facing into the canyon), the lower one would go. When we got to this plateau, off to the left was a herd of goats surrounding an old woman, who sat on a rock, apparently doing nothing but watching the goats. The goats didn't seem to be grazing, as there was only rock there, but they were making quite a bit of noise: bah, bah, bah, in a great chorus that drifted in and out of presenting me with any discernable tone.

We made our way first to the old woman, though purely because she was interesting to the rest of my party, and not because we wanted to (or could) communicate with her. When we got to her, she stared straight ahead with entranced eyes, not looking directly at any of us. The rest of my party began commenting on how interesting she and her goats were, and I and Paul said to her, *"Hola,"* and other phrases of Spanish greeting. She didn't give our greetings any regard; and though it was obvious we found her exceedingly interesting, she didn't seem to find us interesting, but only somehow distressing. Her face was a maze of deep wrinkles on weather-beaten, rough flesh. Her eyes still stared directly forward, their lids having relaxed and settled halfway over their tops, and she didn't seem to even use them to see anything. Her thick body remained perfectly still on the rock.

She began to moan in a low, deep voice—not moaning words, but only a consistent, anguished tone. I had been all along frantically telling the rest of my party we ought to leave her be, and once she started to moan, they finally agreed with me.

We camped not far from her, maybe 200 yards from her in the direction in which the trail descended. There was a little waterspout coming out of the rock of the cliff wall there, from which water came if one turned a knob. The cliff we were on top of was such that our campground was surrounded on three sides by downward slopes that gradually grew more steep, until it became a sheer drop at some point I wasn't about to go and look at. From a little farther down the trail, my father and I looked at our campsite from a little below it, so that we could see the cliff that fell off not far from our tents. The sight of that cliff was overwhelming to my senses. I was overcome by giddiness in looking at it. "How long of a drop is that, do you think?" I asked my father. "Somewhere around a thousand feet, just as a guess," he said. The side of the cliff was red rock that had pronounced vertical lines all along the length of it, until it dropped out of view.

My stepmother, when we went back to our campsite, began wandering down a slope which, I knew, got quickly steeper and steeper until it became that cliff. She often will walk and stand right at the edge of cliffs whenever she is hiking in mountains or canyons, just for the thrill. What she was doing was deeply disturbing to me. She was, after all, so low I couldn't see her, and it was hard to see exactly where the cliff dropped straight down. "Don't do that!" I called to her. "Come back up!" "Don't be silly," she said. "I won't fall." She's acting like a child, I thought, with no conception of danger in the world. "Come back up!" I said. Then I said to her, "It affects me." She finally came up, if only because she didn't want to disturb my mental state further.

That night, I said to my father, "I'm not going farther into the canyon. You can go if you want. I'll stay here and watch the camp." I thought for certain they would go on stupidly offending the Indians, and if they didn't have any idea of the danger we were in, I didn't want to be around them. They would certainly only get me killed.

My father thought it was a good idea. "It sounds like a good plan," he said. "You can watch the tents, and that way we won't have to carry them with us." He could tell I would rather not be there, and wouldn't mind missing out on seeing all those things he found so interesting that lay lower down the trail.

I looked to the dogs, which were near to me, and reached out to pet one of them. He was a yellow mutt with medium-length, matted hair. He was very friendly. "I hope you stay with me tomorrow to keep me company," I said.

18

When I was living in West Los Angeles and going to UCLA, one night I didn't sleep at all, but kept thinking and thinking; so I spent the night writing down my thoughts, until the sensation of sleep-deprivation, around dawn, sent me into an utter calm. I could have easily fallen asleep at that point, but I felt calm and relaxed and kind of dazed, having been up for almost 24 hours, so I wanted to enjoy this feeling for a few more hours. I had a class that started in about 4 hours; but if I stayed up to attend, by then I would completely fall apart mentally, so I decided to miss it.

Around 8:30 in the morning I went to the Sav-On Drugs down the street from where I lived to buy something (I don't remember what), and sat in front of it to wait for it to open. There were a couple of other people waiting with me. One was a buff, good-looking man in his 20s who appeared to be gay. The other was an obviously schizophrenic, fat, ugly woman who kept saying obscene things that did not make any sense. The man in his 20s sat next to me on the bench and asked me for a cigarette, as he saw I was smoking. He said, "I don't normally smoke, but I just worked out." He smiled at me and, as we smoked, we said a few things to each other. I was not averse to flirting with men, which I used to do at times in Los Angeles, when I was younger and more in shape. The woman kept saying obscene things to no one. "What's wrong with this lady?" said the man in his 20s. "She's a crazy lady!" He went on saying other things, right in front of the woman's face, that were very insulting. I was suddenly angry with him, but I didn't say anything; I only began to ignore him. At that moment, I felt so much closer to the fat, ugly woman who kept saying psychotic obscenities, than to the man who dismissed her as a "crazy lady". I wanted to say to him, "I've dealt with your kind all my life. I would much rather live in a place where there are nothing but people like her, than nothing but people like you."

I was just watching part of a TV show as I ate my dinner of Chinese food. I normally only watch TV when I eat my dinner, so I watch less than a half-hour a day. A father was arguing with his daughter about a teen she was dating, on the show on Fox, *Boston Public*. "I know you like him," he said, "but he's a wacko!"

19

There was a problem with staying by our campsite all day. The cliffs. I noticed this once the dogs had followed the rest of my party down the trail. It is that feeling you have when you look over a big drop, which Sartre analyzed in his philosophy on human freedom, that says, "You could jump." And suddenly you are afraid: you really could jump. It would be so easy for me to walk down the steep slope, closer to the cliff, and see what I wanted to do next. This, to me, was the thought that I was afraid of. I didn't want to die. I wasn't suicidal. But I realized that it would be so easy to go down the slope, I could do it any time I wanted. This possibility frightened me; it was Sartre's "vertigo of possibility", though I knew nothing of Sartre then.

I solved this problem by settling on a rock that was a good distance from the cliffs, and saying to myself, "I will not move from this rock, nothing can make me move." One would think I would get bored there. But there was a spectacular view to interest me, to fill me with fear, to overwhelm me with sensation, and I was filled with thoughts that kept coming all day. I spent the day working through these thoughts, "If P then Q, if Q then R," as they formed and reformed in my mind like soldiers going through complicated drills.

Sometimes someone would come by, on his way down the trail. I would speak a few words in Spanish with him, mostly words of greeting, as I explained that I was an American, etc. It didn't occur to me that these men were the "Indians" I had such fear of. They weren't the

"Indians" but ordinary Mexicans who had some sort of business in the canyon. The "Indians" were the ones keeping an eye on me, offended at me, focused on me and my intrusion. These ones could kill me at any time: an arm would sink a hatchet into the back of my head, whose owner I had never heard sneak up on me, and I would never know the difference.

Sometime in the late afternoon the dogs returned. They settled themselves about me and I gave them some food. I would learn later from the others that the dogs had caused them some problems. They had come along a narrow trail to a man driving a bull the opposite way. The dogs had begun to bark at, and even attack, the bull, who had begun to mildly charge back and forth. It was a dangerous situation, so my father and Paul began to beat the dogs with stones to get them to behave. Eventually, the dogs left them and came back to me. I was glad they had, though I didn't at the time know the reason.

I had by now given up on taking extras of my antidepressant. I still thought it was my antipsychotic. I was aware enough to know that I was breaking apart mentally, but my capsules didn't seem to do a thing for me. I was looking forward to getting out of the canyon. Once I was out of the canyon, I would look forward to getting out of Mexico.

20

Two nights later I was in the town of Creel. Since I had refused to travel deeper into the canyon, this had cut our trip short. We had planned on spending four or five nights in the canyon; as it was we spent only two, not counting the night we spend on the canyon rim. So the rest of my party had agreed we would spend at least two nights in the towns surrounding Copper Canyon. Paul and I settled on Creel, while my father and stepmother went on to another town, populated by German immigrants who had settled there generations ago, so that they could see all the things that they found so interesting.

On the train, on the way to Creel, my father sat down next to me. "You don't look like you're doing so good," he said. "What's going on?" "It's Mexico," I said. I refused to elaborate. "What is bothering you?" he said. "It's Mexico," I repeated. I remember sitting there, realizing that the problem wasn't quite Mexico, that the problem was with me, trying to get control of my thoughts, before they ended up in a full-blown delusion. I would say to myself, if the thought crossed my mind that I was a telepath, "No. Don't even consider it. This isn't the place to get psychotic." I simply would not allow myself to fall into the delusion that, had I been under less circumstantial necessity to hold it together, certainly would have taken me over. While my thoughts continued to run, while I was still terrified and thought the Mexicans were after me, I realized on some level that Mexico wasn't the problem, that my mind was the problem. I was resolved to merely go through the motions, to get a hotel, to stay there, to take the train back to Chihuahua City and the bus back to Juarez and then go into El Paso and Texas. Whatever went on in my mind, my physical body would not be affected: my physical body would go through all the actions that were necessary to get me home safely.

There was a hotel in Creel where tourists, many of them native English speakers, stayed. They were mainly backpackers and adventure seekers from places like Australia, the US, and Europe. I chose this hotel, while Paul chose a more expensive one. When it came time to get a room, the girl who was to show me the rooms didn't speak much English. She communicated to me eventually that there were fraternal rooms, where I would be sleeping in bunks with strangers in the same room, or there was one room I could have to my own, for more money. I was confused as she was explaining this, using mostly Spanish, and I began to grow frustrated. I got it across to her that I wanted the room I would have all to my own. She began to explain something

I did not understand. I took it that there was some sort of problem or another, and it might be easier if I took the fraternal room.

I suddenly grew very confused, and under my confusion was a frustration with everything, with the Spanish I did not understand, with the Indians who had sought to kill me, with this dangerous place that was all confusion to me. Suddenly I said to her in English, in almost a scream, "What! what! what!" and then a string of nonsensical syllables, half Spanish, half English, came out of my mouth. I was trying to say: "I don't understand this place, I don't understand what it means, I don't understand what I need to do to survive here, nothing makes sense here. I am so sick of trying to escape danger here; all I want is to survive, and no one will let me." I didn't quite know how to explain this to her, to my father, or to anyone; and so all I could do was to let nonsensical syllables come from my mouth. Then I calmed down, and asked simply, "*¿El cuarto está libre?*"—Is the room free? She replied, "*Sí,*" and without saying another word to me, she led me to my room, handed me the key, and left.

A couple of years ago, my father and I were watching on video the movie, *The Blair Witch Project.* When it got to the part that the woman finds some sort of bizarre wooden object at the door of her tent, my father said to me, "Remember what Donna found at the door of my tent at Copper Canyon?" "No," I said. "There was nothing outside your tent." "That's right," said my father; "you were sleeping, and we thought it would be better not to tell you. You were afraid enough as it was." "What did she find?" I said. "Someone left some sort of doll made of straw and wood," he said. "We found it in the morning." "It's a good thing you didn't show me," I said.

21

Another change in personality. I do not mean I have many personalities. I mean my illness is an illness of personality, so with every new medication I try, my personality is altered. I do not always want a new personality; sometimes I will say, "I want to be me, not someone else," but then my psychosis will make me miserable enough to try one.

I am no longer writing as a psychotic symptom. I do not now write all day, but it is in fact a little difficult to become motivated to write. This is because I came off my Loxapine and went back on Haldol. In addition, I have a regular dose of Risperdal that I have kept constant. These are all antipsychotics. That's the only type of medication I need.

The second day of my switch back to Haldol I straightened my apartment, did my dishes and cleaned my sink, and took a shower. I had not taken a shower in about six days. I looked myself in the mirror, ran a hand through my hair, and said to myself, "I would really like a shower." I did not say this on Loxapine.

I am not now satisfied with sitting and thinking all day, but my mind is calmer; so I have been smoking less, and reading more. I have a normal appetite back, which is bad news in a sense because I had a lot more extra money when I was eating only one meal a day. The trade off? I have more anxiety. I can't sleep at night. When I do fall asleep, I cannot wake up till eleven or twelve hours later. My stomach inflammation is back, and I throw up as soon as I awake every morning. I have an appointment with my doctor tomorrow. He doesn't know yet that I went back on Haldol. We'll have to see what can be done.

22

When I was in a hospital in Los Angeles (I was 18 or 19) there was a gay man who was my roommate. He was in his 30s, but if he was attracted to me, he obviously considered me too young for him. One night the staff drove him and the rest of us to an AA meeting for male gays. There was another meeting for straights in the same building, but I thought it would be interesting to go to the one for gays. I told myself, "There is nothing wrong with being gay; though I am not gay I will not shun them. I'll go to the meeting for gays." There was one young man there in particular I kept staring at. His eyes had a similar look to mine—over stimulated with sensation, only his held a certain degree of excitement. One could look at him and have the sense that his eyes were simply overflowing with sight.

There was another man I got to talking to there—I don't remember his name so let's call him Carver. Carver was slightly overweight and not particularly attractive. But he seemed friendly enough, and he had 5 years sobriety, so I asked him to be my AA sponsor. He accepted, and very gladly. We exchanged numbers.

I still didn't see the social significance of our exchanging of numbers. There we were, in an AA meeting for gays, exchanging numbers with one another. One of us soon called the other, and he picked me up for a meeting. Over the next few months, we went to many meetings together—I had no idea he might be attracted to me, and be under the impression I was attracted to him. I never presented myself as available to him at all. He never made a move on me, but dropped me little hints. Once, he lent me the AA book, *Twelve Steps, Twelve Traditions*. As I was reading it later, I noticed a single, curly pubic hair lodged in its pages.

At the meetings he took me to, I tried to get dates with women (these were all straight meetings). I was never successful, but this all probably seemed very strange to him. One day he said to me, "Why did you go to the meeting we met at?" I didn't quite understand; I said I went along with a friend. "But why that meeting?" he said.

Soon, he started to set me up with his gay friends; he knew I was schizophrenic, and probably felt sorry for me; and though he was no longer interested in me, he did not want to give me the cold shoulder.

After all, he was my sponsor now. He would tell me a certain friend could give me a ride home from a particular meeting, and his friend and I would go to the friend's apartment first and talk. With one of these friends, we exchanged our writing, as he was a writer also. Looking back on it, I can see all the significance this had for the others; but at the time, I was oblivious to it. So I never made myself available to be approached sexually, and I never was.

I lost my virginity at 14, and then I kind of said to myself, "Well that's over with; now I don't have to pursue any relationships." There was a kind of cultural pressure about and significance in losing one's virginity; I didn't want to be a loser who was still a virgin at 16. But I did not make love again until I was 20. That too was a short-term fling, one I actually desired and wanted to develop into a relationship. But the woman left me, and though I have dated, I haven't so much as kissed another human being since. I think if I did, I would only run as fast as I could, man, or woman.

23

You may ask yourself at some point in this narrative, "Why does he believe these strange delusions? If he is intelligent and can think logically, what convinces him of all this?" I can only reply by saying to you that it is like when you suspect something about a situation that you really cannot know. Say you go on a first date and he says he'll call; the next day you get a call and the person hangs up on you. Some people might wonder if this is your date, might even go over the date and pick out something in the man's or woman's personality that would indicate such a behavior. If you find something that does, and the hang-up calls continue, you might begin to suspect it is your date. A psychotic belief is similar to this—only the belief is more than a suspicion, it becomes so much stronger and complex and involved. Every part fits in logically with every other part—it is a belief system as involved and complex as the belief system we call "Catholicism". It takes on a sense of complete reality, so that every experience is interpreted in its terms, and seems to support it. I began with this very mystery, this question, "Why does an intelligent schizophrenic believe such absurd things?" in the philosophical essay I mentioned earlier, and my theory that served as an answer took 140 pages to explicate. For now, just understand that it is a mystery, even to the schizophrenic.

24

When I had my first psychotic breakdown, beginning just before my 17th birthday, I believed everyone in the room, no matter where I was, could hear my thoughts, and see in their mind's eye the images that passed though my own. This was probably the time of the worst mental anguish of my life. I remember shortly before my actual birthday, just days after school started, when I was tripping acid with my friends. I was outside my father's house, walking through the suburban, residential neighborhoods that surrounded it. There were many areas of these housing developments that were like parks, my father's neighborhood filled with manmade ponds with wooden bridges over them in places, making it easy to walk to wherever one was going. I was walking near one of these bridges, thinking about my upcoming birthday, how my grandparents and the rest of my family would be there and how, with my newly gained telepathic powers, it could only end in disaster. Of course, my friend Frederick knew perfectly what was on my mind. "Are you looking up at future challenges?" he said to me. I mumbled a response, but made my main response with my mind.

Later that night, I tried to climb onto the flat roof over my father's garage. I often did this whenever I was locked out; it was very easy for me to climb up there, and get in through a window. But now I was completely delirious and my friends could not control me. I wasn't planning on jumping, but there was no telling what would come into my mind once I was up there; and I could easily, in that state, fall. My friend Frederick, once I had grabbed a hold of the handhold I needed to swing my legs up, immediately threw his arms around my waist, and began to pull me as hard as he could. I suddenly didn't know where I was or what situation I was in, but because of my LSD hallucinations thought I was floating through space, the angels holding onto my hands from above, the whole human race holding onto my body from below. Then, all at once, I lost my grip, and found myself by my father's door, my friends running away from a car that had just pulled up. (They thought it was a cop; it was only my father's roommate.) My pants had been pulled down below my waist so that I had to, embarrassed, pull them back up and fix my belt. Back to earth. It was a rude awakening.

25

I spent the night in my king-sized waterbed, with my clothes on, next to my friend Leo, who had only taken half a hit. When the car had pulled up that everyone thought was a cop, he had gotten my key, and opened the door to my father's house, then led me inside and up to my room. My father was sleeping soundly in his own room; it was the early morning (2:00 or 3:00 a.m.), and he had to work the next day.

As I was lying down for the night, I believed I was going off into the spirit world forever; there was no need to take care that material things would be provided for. So I took off my contact lenses, and instead of placing them in their container, I merely threw them aside, somewhere on the bed, and lay back to enter the spirit world once and for all. The next day, it would take me hours to find them.

I hallucinated on the bed next to Leo all night. We both had our clothes on, and the bed was more than big enough for both of us.

I didn't get any sleep all night. In the morning, my father knocked on my door and told me to get ready for school. I ignored him until he became more and more insistent, and then went into the shower and shut the door. I took a very long shower. By the time I was done, my father had gone to work.

Meanwhile, Leo (who I believe actually slept a few hours) got up and began to get ready to leave. I went back into bed once my father was gone, and slept probably two hours. By the time I was awake again, and no longer having LSD hallucinations, Leo was gone.

Later that day, as I was alone at home, I looked out past my father's patio and saw a man who looked much like me, but older. He was apparently homeless, and had all sorts of religious talismans and charms hanging from his body. He was crouching on the grass, his knees at his chest, his buttocks nearly touching the ground. He seemed to be under some sort of spell that made it difficult for him to know where he was, what he was doing. He was ritualistically moving his arms over the grass, in some sort of sacrament I did not understand.

I thought to myself, "That is I, from the future, having come to bless the spot where I had the vision last night." I stared at him for a few moments, then went and did something else. When I came back a second time, he was still there. When I came back the third time, he was gone. I never saw him again.

26

My 17th birthday celebration consisted of my mother, stepfather, sister, and my mother's parents. Though I wasn't high and had taken no drugs that day, I was certain everyone in the room could hear my thoughts, and see the images that passed through my mind's eye. It was like this for me all the time, even if I went a week without so much as drinking a beer or smoking marijuana. This reality—the telepathic reality of my experience—would not abate.

I, like most young men from the time they hit puberty, had a certain sense of "sacredness" in my grandmother, such that my grandmother was to hear no foul language from my mouth, or any sexual suggestiveness; and if she did, I had a great sense of shame. But when I thought she could hear my thoughts, I tried to control those thoughts, to stop her from hearing sexually obscene thoughts or seeing in her mind's eye sexually obscene images. It is common knowledge that if one is in any way aware of what one must not think, one will immediately think it. I did not see the futility in trying to control my thoughts; I was so ashamed of them that I knew I must control them, and there was no other option. So I was left lost in a sea of sexual images having to do with my grandmother, the very images that would offend her the most. I was convinced that she knew precisely what was passing through my mind, that everyone in the room did, and that they were all doing their best to ignore it.

But my grandmother wasn't very good at ignoring it. After one particularly disturbing image had passed through my mind's eye, she said to me, "That sounds like a hint!" in a biting tone, at least as biting a tone as she ever used, which was rare for her. I immediately stood up and walked away into the other room; all I wanted was for this night to be over, for everyone to leave, so that I could be alone, and no longer have to try to control my thoughts. But I couldn't escape: I had to go through the dinner, the eating of cake and the blowing out of its candles, the opening of presents, every ten minutes of which was an agony I felt I could not bear.

Finally, my grandparents left. As my grandfather was saying goodbye to me, he shook my hand, and said, "Hang in there." I always got the sense when he said this that he knew somehow that life had become agony for me, and was trying to do all he could to help, which wasn't much. But he would do what he could do—tell me, "Hang in there," as if to say, "I too was once your age, and I too have suffered before, and look how long I have survived." Of course, he had never been psychotic, but certainly he had suffered in his own way, gone through his own trials, such as occur in every human life, rich or poor, mentally ill or mentally healthy. He said this phrase, "Hang in there," to me every time he saw me now, though he never said it before I became psychotic, and never said it after I was well on my way to stability.

27

How did this telepathic phenomenon start? How did I first begin to notice it, and how did I become convinced of it? The following experiences are an explanation.

First of all, it needs to be told that I was somewhat of a hoodlum as a teen. I hung out with the wrong crowd, and none of us did well in school, all of us drug addicts. I was once placed under arrest for a second-degree burglary, because of an impulsive act of theft of one of the friends I had been with a few nights before. When I explained to the police precisely what had happened, and gave them the name of the one who had done the job, they left me alone, and never bothered me about it again. I sometimes wonder where I would have ended up had I never become mentally ill, and thus been taken away from the influence of those friends.

One time, before I was quite psychotic, I spent the day with my friends snorting meth-amphetamine. I normally didn't do speed, as it wasn't to my taste, but this day I indulged. Late that night, I ended up in my room at my father's house with my friend Leo, who needed a place to crash. We did a couple more lines, smoked some pot, and then lay down with our clothes on, on my massive bed. As I was lying next to him, I found that I was too wired from the crystal meth, and couldn't sleep. I lay on my back, staring up, not tossing and turning because I didn't want to disturb him, but perfectly still. Sometime during the night, I began to become more aware of him, and aware also of certain sexual fantasies of images of women. I somehow took it for a given that he could see the fantasies too. I thought it would be interesting to lie on my back, and picture making love to a woman with her on top of me, so that, as she rode me, he could see all this also.

Of course, I had no notion that this could be considered a homo-erotic situation. To be gay, among my society, was what it would be to be a child molester in our society at large. It was the worst thing in the world, to be gay, and no one even considered that homosexuality could, on any possible defense, be acceptable. On the contrary, to call a rock song or public personality gay, was an argument in itself—it needed no defending that gayness was itself a terrible crime and perversion.

So I went on picturing women on top of me, with increasing detail, taking it as perfectly natural that Leo saw the women in his mind's eye too. Everything I saw with my eyes others saw—this was perfectly natural, though I needed no rational arguments to learn it. So also, it seemed a perfectly natural proposition that Leo saw what was in my mind's eye. And fantasizing about women could never be gay. Such a thought seemed absurd.

I thought somehow that it would impress Leo greatly if I worked my way up into an ejaculation without ever touching myself. My fantasies had made me fully erect, but my erection was covered over by the comforters, and I knew enough to realize it would be very inappropriate to actually touch myself. I never found the fantasies stimulating enough to ejaculate, but I tried, and I thought somehow that Leo would be amazed at my mental powers if I had.

The next day, I was back to normal. It had only been a passing notion that Leo could see what was in my mind's eye. I didn't look back and wonder what I had been thinking; I took it for a given that Leo had seen the women, but I didn't think it was important enough to pursue, or that I had the ability to bring on this telepathy at just any time. I never asked him what he knew about the situation.

28

I imagine you're still unconvinced. Why would I take it for a given that Leo knew what went on in my own fantasies? This is not, after all, "perfectly natural", but completely alien to all our experience. Something else was needed to dissolve the distinction between inner mind and outer world for me, some earlier experience was needed to teach me that this was not quite a solid distinction.

The first time it occurred to me. This was when I was first beginning to really explore LSD, and the inner worlds it opened up for me. I heedlessly opened up my own psychology, and permanently damaged it in the process, all in order to explore its mysteries.

My friend Frederick was acquainted with a dishwasher in his 20s named Don. Don was uneducated and lived from check to check, in order to maintain his small, one bedroom apartment. He was able to afford the inexpensive luxuries that bring those of his class pleasure and relaxation—TV, furniture, guitar equipment, a stereo and music, a cheap car and gasoline, a daily dose of marijuana, beer for the days off work. This, I believe, is something like the life I would be leading now had I never become mentally ill. I feel, actually, though I am just as poor, that I am better off how I am; but of course that's all speculation. My life, had I never become schizophrenic, would be so radically different from how it is, it's futile to try to imagine it, and come to any real conclusions.

One night, Frederick, Don and I took LSD at Don's apartment. Earlier that night, as the drug had just begun to take effect, we had been walking through a park where there were various structures for children to play in. It was late and there were no children. We climbed up into one of these structures, which was something like a very tall rocket, with walls that were made of thin metal bars, such that no children that high in the air could fall out of it. As soon as we were at the top, Don and Frederick began to rock the structure back and forth, so that it swayed in the air, and appeared to be about to fall at any second. I was terrified, and told them to stop; but the more I complained, the harder they laughed and shook it, so I had to withstand my terror of falling in silence, or otherwise there would be no end to it.

Later that night, as we sat in Don's apartment listening to music and tripping, my LSD having taken full effect, I saw hallucinations of various images coming out of the walls. LSD hallucinations are not at all like psychotic hallucinations. LSD takes what is already there, and distorts it, by causing sights to metamorphose, and colors and shades to change in degree of brightness and darkness. The actual images of human figures or geometric forms that come are always like cartoons, made of colorful light, that have a certain degree of "unreality" in their impression on the mind. Psychotic visual hallucinations, on the other hand, have precisely the same appearance as things one sees in one's everyday life. They appear to the mind just the same way as a man or woman appears in the sight of a normal person, who is not on drugs, and has his senses in no way distorted. I was not seeing any psychotic hallucinations at the time, but only ones from the LSD.

The images that were appearing to me were very sensual. I was only 16, and very repressed; it only makes sense that my unconscious would dwell on sex, given the opportunity to express itself. I saw images of men and women in sensual activities, the actual images and situations constantly changing, never for a moment still; I could not see them clearly. But I was seeing these things; they weren't in my mind's eye, but actually in my field of vision. I began to grow ashamed of the images, and with the shame grew a growing self-consciousness that told me the others could see what I was seeing. Their conversation didn't make proper sense to me, but more and more made sense only in terms of my own inner subjectivity, thought, and hallucinations. I began to take it as perfectly natural that what I saw with my eyes they saw just the way I did. I was, after all, actually seeing these things.

But on some level I knew the images came from my imagination. Whatever my train of thought was working through, the images matched it. Whatever I began to fear to see, out of a sense of shame, I began to see more of. Thus did this distinction between what went on in my own imagination, and what others were aware of, begin to dissolve. It sort of worked this way. 1) What I see others see (a perfectly natural assumption). 2) I see what comes from my own imagination (the LSD caused this phenomenon). Therefore: others see what comes from my own imagination. If I ever doubted in this reasoning, I would involuntarily be sent back into it by a sense of shame. The images would turn sexual, and whether I believed consciously the others saw them or not, I was ashamed of them, and thus I was sent into assuming the others saw them by an emotion. Rather than reason convincing me the others probably didn't see them, my fear that they did was too great to be overcome by reasoning that said they didn't.

This feeling wore off with the LSD, however. Later, if I looked back on this experience, I took it as real: the others had actually seen my hallucinations. But after the LSD wore off, I was no longer troubled by it, at least for a few more weeks.

But I never asked them directly if they had seen my hallucinations, but began to withdraw into myself, never mentioning what was on my mind. I had learned over the years to keep my feelings to myself from the strict social norms of my particular society. Someone who said something impertinent or foolish was ridiculed, no one wanted to appear as if he didn't fit in or was someone "uncool", and any sexual feeling or weakness of emotions outside certain parameters was immediately denounced as completely perverse, disgusting and abnormal. So over the years I had learned to put on an appearance of fitting in, though my inner self did not actually fit in, and therefore I learned that it must be repressed, hidden from the others, and never expressed with words or behavior. Thus had I learned over the years to keep my feelings and personal troubles inside of me. I would only amplify this containment as the months of psychosis wore on.

29

I still remember the day it happened. The day I awoke, completely sober, and believed others could hear my thoughts.

I had been tripping LSD with my friends Leo and Al the night before. Al was older than us, around 19 or 20, and he didn't go to our high school. He was the one who had gotten me arrested for a second-degree burglary. He was fun enough to be around, but you didn't want to get on his bad side (I was 6′2″ and he was a few inches taller than me, and weighed well over 200 pounds, though he wasn't obese). Had the police actually contacted him after I gave them his name and told them what he did, I don't know what he may have done; but the police seemed to forget about the whole thing once I explained to them what had happened, and didn't pursue it.

I remember one day I and Al had been playing around, sort of play-fighting in the street, and I had thrown several blows at his face, without ever making contact. This was my way of saying, "I could have hit you with every one of those punches." His response was to reach around me, lift me up off my feet and over his head, and then set me down gently. This was his way of saying, "I could have thrown your body down on the pavement, and there would have been nothing you could do."

Somehow, we ended up at one of Al's friend's apartments. It was in a seedy neighborhood, and there were two others there besides us, who had taken no LSD, and would only drink beer the whole night. This was the first time I had met these two friends of Al. They seemed to want to spend their night "tripping us out" by their conversation. I didn't want to stay there, but I didn't really have a choice: Leo had said he would drive us home, as I didn't want to drive in my state, and Leo had taken less of the drug than I.

As we were watching TV, there was a movie on I had never seen, some second-rate action film. There was a car on a bridge, and its driver was shooting at someone, who was firing back. One of Al's friends said, "Hey Al, that guy in the car reminds me of Alex Green—the guy with the skin disease who always sat so still." I looked down at my arms. My skin was very blotchy, with patches of red and other patches that were pale, and I had been sitting awkwardly still all night. "You mean the tall blond Alex, or the shorter guy with dark hair?" This was Al's way of asking if his friend were referring to Leo—shorter with dark hair—or me—tall with blond hair. "No, the tall bond guy," said Al's friend. "You know who I mean." Suddenly I realized Al's friend had identified me with the man in the car, who was being shot at. Just then the car was hit in the wrong place, and it exploded in a great burst of flame. "Damn!" said Al. "If I had been in that car, I would have just gotten the hell out of there."

I realized this talk was all suggestive, almost metaphorical. There was a covert meaning to everything everybody said. This type of talk was what I would later (once hospitalized) tell my therapist were the "metaphors" I heard in conversation—words didn't mean what they ostensibly did, but stood for a secret meaning, which was never overtly discussed, but only "understood" by all parties.

This was the first time I had ever been introduced to such an idea—the idea that words could be used to suggest things, without overtly stating their meaning. I began to join in on the conversation, to defend myself using these "metaphors", and to insult the others. The complexity of the secret meaning grew and grew, and the best "secret meaning" was one in which all understood the suggested meaning, but one could never find any deviation from a natural way of expressing the ostensible meaning.

As I joined in and used secret meaning, the others seem to think I was very good at insulting the others using it. They said things like,

"He wails," which was our slang for, "He is good at insulting people in clever ways." Whenever someone had particularly insulted someone else, we would say, "He was wailing on him."

This was the last piece of the puzzle of my psychosis that needed to fall into place. After this point, wherever I was, whomever I was with, whether listening to a lecture in class, or listening to music with my friends, it would seem like this secret meaning was in everything everyone said. What were they really talking about? They were talking about my mental content—the thoughts and images that went through my mind. This was when I began to withdraw completely into myself, and be incapable of any meaningful communion with another mind—everything that person said would be perceived by me as meaning something completely different from what was really intended.

30

My father came by today. Just before leaving, he used the toilet. After he had been gone about 15 minutes, I noticed that the toilet tank was still refilling after he had flushed it. I took off the porcelain top of the tank and noticed the chain that attaches the rubber stopper at the bottom, over the hole through which the water drains, to the handle one pushes to flush the toilet, had become unattached. I reattached it, and that solved the problem. A healthy mind would regard this as a perfectly "random" incident with no specific significance. But I didn't understand it at all. That chain had worked fine for years, without ever becoming unattached, and then my father uses the toilet once, and it becomes unattached. This did not make sense to me. I immediately found myself thinking, "He took the chain off on purpose—he has some plan to do some harm." Were I not on medication, I would obsess about this little "random" incident until it was only one part in a complex, interconnected, comprehensible belief system—a psychotic delusion. This is how delusions start, with significance seen in experiences that to healthy minds have no significance. Since I cannot comprehend my experiences, I render them comprehensible with psychotic belief systems.

31

I first became psychotic, as I have said, just before I turned 17. But long before that, when I was only 15, I had certain social difficulties. In those days I had a friend named Ramsey and I often got together with him, his girlfriend, and some of her friends, especially a Chinese American one named Amy. It was my freshman year in high school, and I knew all these people from school, though Ramsey and I had known each other since as far back as the 4th grade in elementary school.

We rarely did anything stronger than pot when we got together, but often drank hard liquor in addition. When we got together, we would sit around the TV, stoned or drunk, and talk all night, or sometimes we drove around town. I remember quite distinctly my self-consciousness as I was watching TV with them. Was it considered a "strange look of staring" to constantly look into the TV? I somehow thought it was, so instead of looking straight at the TV, I would pick a spot to the lower left of it, and stare at that. I didn't, after all, want to look like I kept staring in the same place. Was it considered "strange looking" to walk always with the same motion of the arms? I thought so, so I would walk usually with no motion in my arms. What did motion in the arms accomplish when walking anyway? Did it seem strange to people if you stared at their faces? It seemed like it to me. I would pick a spot behind the person, usually a little lower than the face and off to the left or right, while I was speaking. If I were speaking to a group of people at once, such as when our little group was together, stoned and watching TV, I would pick some spot on the wall, and stare at that as I spoke. Thus I became known as "weird", which is the high school equivalent of eccentric; but certain high school students actually liked "weird" people, because they were different and not like everyone else, and so my good friends did not shun me, or make any fun at my eccentricities.

32

Three months after late July of 1989, after the day I woke up one day and went through my life believing everyone around me could hear my thoughts, I was admitted to my first psychological hospital.

Before that, I had no realistic conception of what was happening to me. My father had bought a book (I don't remember the name of the author) called *Way of the Shaman* years earlier. It was by an anthropologist who had studied the shamanism of tribal people in South America (the Yanomamo in particular), and had become, in the view of the tribes, a shaman himself. The book wasn't an ethnography or anthropological work, however; it was more a New Age, practical guidebook on how to become a shaman. I picked up this book after I had gained my telepathic powers, and it became a Bible for me: I religiously went through the creative visualization exercises it prescribed. I thought my new powers had something to do with spirits; I had seen and communicated with what I took for spirits on LSD, and I believed they had given me these new mental powers I found myself with. I was sure that if I ever were to learn to control these powers, it would be through shamanic exercises.

From the time school started in early September, until late October when I was admitted to the hospital (though this is only two months, to me it seemed, and still seems, like a very long time), my best friend was Frederick. He lived in my neighborhood, and my father drove us both to school on his way to work every morning. We took the same bus back from school, and he would normally come over to my place with me to smoke some pot and listen to music with me. When we got to my place on those days he was with me, he understood that I had to first listen to the tape I had made of drumming in the dark bathroom, and go into the "underworld" of creative visualization. He never asked what I was doing in there. He understood that I was into shamanism; he thought it must be similar to the way in which his other friend, whom I mentioned before, Don, was into the Necronomicon.

Once I was over at Don's apartment with Frederick and some others. It was a party of sorts, though it was a small group of people. We were all drinking beer and having a good time (except for me, who was dealing with my thoughts). There were some others in the kitchen but for some reason they were moving on into Don's bedroom, and Frederick sat on the living room couch as I stood there in the same room. Frederick was calling loudly to the others, talking in an excited tone, trying to make a point that seemed to particularly affect him at the moment. He said something like, "Just think what we'd be like if we took 5 hits of acid right now! You know what we'd be like? Can you imagine it? We'd even be like Jason is now!" I wasn't on acid, but only drunk. Frederick suddenly realized that the others hadn't heard him, that I was in fact the only one who had heard him. He felt bad. "Sorry," he said. "Sometimes you forget who you're talking to."

At another time, Frederick and I were in my room in my father's house. We had smoked some pot earlier, and it was late. I had a TV in there, and we had been watching it all evening. My thoughts had been wandering all night, in a constant dialogue with Frederick, as I examined myself and tried to explain myself to Frederick telepathically. My thoughts were wandering from this to that, and I really wasn't aware of what was on TV, but only what I was explaining to Frederick and at the same time examining myself with my mind. I was doing so with both thoughts and images, as I often communicated to others in these days with creative images seen in my mind's eye.

When Frederick stood up to leave, he said to me, "I put on Simon & Garfunkel's Greatest Hits the other night, and it just *played*." I thought he meant that he had enjoyed listening to my thoughts play and play, and had found the playing of my thoughts and images particularly entertaining and interesting that night. I responded with a couple words to this effect, though I acted as if we both understood I had telepathy and mustn't overtly discuss it, and didn't spell it out for him what I meant. "What?" he said. "What do you mean?" This was a shock to me. I certainly had responded to my friends in ways they didn't understand before during that time, but they had never called me on it; they had simply ignored it. I don't know what made him decide not to ignore it that time, but this incongruity of my experience with my delusion wasn't strong enough to tear down the delusion itself; I went back to believing others knew my thoughts as soon as he was gone.

33

As the school year was finishing up in the spring of 1989, and I was just finishing my sophomore year, I had a sense that something magical lay ahead for me in the summer. I quit my job washing dishes during that time, and to this day I am not sure why. I didn't come to the decision because of "reasons"; all I know is that one day I gave my boss two weeks notice. I had worked that job weekends, Saturday and Sunday, for two years, and I was very good at it. I would sleep in and miss the first part of school; but though I had to be at that breakfast restaurant to wash dishes at 7:00 a.m., I was never late.

I remember going on a hiking trip with my father just as school was ending. I was looking forward to the summer. I was looking forward to the rest of my life. I sat on the edge of some small Utah canyon or gulch, listening to a tape of music on my boom box, and said to my father something like, "Isn't this music great? Doesn't it capture such a feeling of beauty and hope? Doesn't it capture perfectly the experience of sitting here, in this canyon, with all this beauty around us?" There was nothing, it seemed, that more perfectly captured my happiness than that song I was playing, "Summertime Rolls," by Jane's Addiction. I was looking forward to the summer, and all the magic it would open up for me. I had a sense that something great would happen to me that summer. I had only recently begun exploring LSD, and I was looking forward to that, this summer, too.

The rest of my life lay ahead of me, and I was so happy sitting in that Utah wilderness, listening to my favorite music, that I could only see a hopeful future ahead. I had a sense that this very summer was when my life would really begin.

34

When I was in elementary school, in the fifth grade, I became very interested in the magic of witchcraft. There seemed a mystery about witchcraft, and I thought somehow that if I investigated the right sources, I would be able to find magical powers. The only real book on witchcraft in the school library, though, was one on the Salem witch trials, and all their history. I read that book cover to cover, and I was somehow disappointed that the witches in Salem weren't real witches, with real magical powers.

One day, as we stood on the risers for our class photograph, I got it into my head that I could cause the film to blur through sheer mental ability. I concentrated with all my might: I focused on the camera, and sent a very powerful feeling of deep concentration and mental energy upon its sight. I thought to myself, "The shot will come out blurred when they develop it, and then I'll know for sure that it was I who did it with my mind."

When the photograph came back and was mounted on the wall and sent to all the parents, it wasn't blurred, however. But off in the back row, at the right end, was a tall little boy with a bizarre stare in his eyes, a very fixed and almost tormented gaze. He seemed to stand out as having a very unusual expression, especially for a photograph in which everyone was smiling. His lips were stone and pressed together, without the slightest hint of happy expression; but the strangest part of his face was his eyes. They seemed to say, "I am not with the rest of you; I am different."

35

I think this project is starting to get to me. All this dwelling on my past, thinking about the good and the bad, writing mostly the bad. Last night I had a dream that my brother went to meet some people about checking himself into a mental hospital (he has never been in one, in real life, except to visit me). I went with him to meet the people, and we met in a rail yard. There were two men and one short woman. The short woman said, "Let me tell you: if you give your consent to enter my hospital, I will have the power to subject you to physical takedowns, all sorts of punishments, and seclusion." My brother said, "I do not give my consent." Suddenly all three of them jumped on him and began to subdue him to carry him off to the hospital. I said to them, "I was a witness! He did not give his consent!" then I ran away in terror. They chased me along the train tracks and tackled me. The next thing I knew I was in the mental hospital. I did not see my brother; I was told he was in seclusion, and would not submit to their control of him, so he was being punished. I kept looking for an opportunity to escape. Finally, I found myself on a football field near my high school. The football players were going through their drills. There was a mental health worker from the hospital with me; this was only some sort of outing, and they were watching me to make sure I didn't escape. I tried to make my escape. Just as the football players were rushing in my direction, I went with the flow of their motion, and began to run away. It was almost like waves at the seashore, the football players rushing in, and rushing out, just as the water at the sea rolls in and recedes. I made my move when they were rushing with me, in the direction I had to run, so that they would mask my escape. I found myself then walking along with a mustached policeman on one side and a male mental health worker on the other. The mental health worker was saying, "Mustache cop, mustache cop, this guy is trying to escape from a mental hospital; help me capture him." The mustached policeman wouldn't listen to him, but only made suggestive comments to him, very crude come-ons.

36

So I went through it: I went through my daily routine, my classes in school, meetings with my mother, stepfather, and father, getting together with friends; I went through all that. I was apathetically going along with it, though the presence of people was a torment to me. I was trying to control my thoughts, all day long I was desperately trying to avoid thoughts that humiliated me.

Every day I fell into the same pattern of thoughts. Disgusting sexual images would come into my mind due to the mere act of trying to force them not to. Then I would defend myself with other thoughts: I was trying to convince everyone I wasn't gay. The thoughts I tried to avoid suggested I was gay. I realize this sounds petty, even immature; but I was in a social environment that said to entertain plans to rob a liquor store with a loaded gun was cool, but to be gay was unforgivable. Furthermore, my friends mostly all had girlfriends: the closest I had come to that was when I had lost my virginity, and I hadn't followed up on it with a relationship. I was good-looking enough; some girls tried to form a bond with me; but I was so afraid of any type of intimacy that I became apathetic toward them.

The one thing I would have a hard time dealing with, once I was on medication and my major psychosis left me, was that a very strong relationship of mine was only a delusion. She was a real person—an English teacher of mine whom I called by her first name, Lydia, when I spoke to her with my thoughts—but the entire relationship I formed with her was only in my mind.

Schizophrenics are less able than normies to perceive what interpersonal interactions actually mean, what is intended by gestures and the look in someone's eyes, even comments and suggestions. When a man and a woman are flirting together, they sort of "intuit" the sensual understanding between them: they do not state it overtly most of the time. Thus, over the years I have had a very hard time being able to tell when a situation is romantic, and when it is completely unromantic. In my psychotic state, I believed Lydia was amazed at my telepathic power, that she wanted me to rescue her from a stale marriage with my passionate love for her and my mysterious gift. I had not yet learned, as I learned later, not to trust my "intuition" of a romantic situation. Now, it would take a woman actually saying, "Kiss me you fool," for me to actually kiss her; and this has led to several dates in which we had a good time but later parted ways without so much as a handshake.

I never tried to kiss Lydia. I tried to romance her with my thoughts. I told her how much I loved her. I went on and on about it. I would work through my thoughts; my thoughts would move through my mind in complex patterns like a marching band on a football field, constantly creating new formations and arrangements; and this was all in dialogue with Lydia: I was romancing Lydia. I, like the narrator in James Joyce's "Araby", was the knight there to rescue her from her drab everyday life, and take her on the adventure my magical powers would provide.

Thus, even when alone at home, drifting off to sleep, I would not be at peace, but would be dialoguing with Lydia. Every waking hour I spent in my telepathic world. When I was walking home from the bus stop, and alone, I was in contact with Lydia, speaking with her, interacting with her. When I was in class or with my family or friends, I was trying to control my thoughts, trying to avoid the thoughts that humiliated me, trying to convince them I wasn't gay, trying to explain the obscene images that passed through my mind. Such was the agony that would have lasted, were it not for medication, thirteen years, on into the present.

One day I was in the office of my American History teacher (Mrs. Clifton, not Lydia). I had had this teacher for social studies the year previous, and had done very well. I was there to see another teacher who shared her office, the teacher of a class on world religions who was new to me. They were in there talking to each other and to me. "Mrs. Clifton tells me you're very intelligent," said the world religions teacher. I kind of mumbled, "I...I..." until they changed the subject. I wanted to say, "I used to be."

At another time, as I was making my way through the crowded halls of my high school, suddenly my school counselor appeared right in front of me. I had had trouble with my grades in past years, though intelligence tests had showed I had the capability to soar in school. This counselor took a special interest in getting me signed up for classes I would find more interesting, so that I would be motivated to apply myself. But when he appeared before me now, he put his hands on my shoulders, a grave expression on his face, and said, "Jason! If there's anything you need to talk about, come see me. Please, come and see me!" I nodded to him, without saying a word, making my response to him with my mind, and walked on. Within seconds, he had disappeared back into the crowd.

37

I went and picked up my medication today. I realized when I got home how much medication I have. My doctor recently called in the higher dosage prescription of Loxapine, and though I had plenty of the Loxapine left from my refill of the lower dosage, I went ahead and picked up the new prescription along with my refill of Risperdal today. Now, I have plenty of Loxapine, and I am very happy about it. I can take extras whenever I want. It has a sedative effect, like Haldol, and I enjoyed taking extras of Haldol when I was on that too. It makes me, basically, numb. I do not feel bad; I do not feel good; I am just *existing*, and it is a calm, undisturbed, drowsy existence.

It was good to get out of my apartment for the walk to the pharmacy. It feels good to go anywhere where the people you are dealing with know you are schizophrenic, and usually they do not treat you badly. I don't like being around people and thinking to myself, "I have to keep my schizophrenia a secret; it would make people uncomfortable if I told them." It's much easier if one is in a hospital, or picking up medication, or visiting one's doctor in the outpatient clinic, where it is understood, "He is schizophrenic" and no one needs to say it or keep it secret.

When I told my high school friends of my illness, the ones who were very bad influences anyway, they began to shun me socially, which actually worked out well, because my illness doesn't mix with that lifestyle. But I had one friend in those days, named Joe, who even visited me in the hospital. Now, he's the only friend I know who lives in Denver, outside of family. He is married to one of my pharmacists. Don't think I am somehow the link between these two: he met her before she was a pharmacist, and she ended up working at my pharmacy through pure coincidence. When I was in Los Angeles and learning Spanish, I grew fond of Mexican norteña and other styles of Mexican music, so last summer Joe, his wife (my pharmacist), my brother and I went to see, on my suggestion, Los Tigres del Norte play at Mile High Stadium. It feels good to associate with people who know perfectly well that I'm schizophrenic. I hate hiding it from people, and having to pretend it's not there, in me, an intimate part of me.

I'm on the burly side, and when I go about the city, I dress somewhat like a street person. I'm comfortable that way: my clothes are dirty, I haven't showered in a few days, I wear cheap, worn sneakers and a coat warm enough for much colder weather. I find that dressing this way says to people: Keep away. That way, I feel perfectly comfortable going through bad neighborhoods, and I feel like I fit in when I see others out there similar to me. Wealthier people in my neighborhood are comfortable around people like me: there are enough of us around, and they have grown used to it. I feel like I fit into my surroundings, into society, going about the way I do. I don't fit in with the wealthier people, the health nuts who work in offices and ride their bikes or jog through Washington Park, who are seen in Einstein's Bagels or Starbucks in the morning, but I don't need to. When there are enough of us not like these people, enough who are "different" in a given area, "different" becomes rendered more normal.

38

The concept of black pride does not come from any notion that blacks are superior to whites. It comes from black shame—the fact that blacks have been taught for generations to be ashamed of being black. And so black pride becomes necessary. The same thing is necessary for mental illness. Certainly it seems strange to be proud to have a disabling disease. But I still cannot introduce myself to a university creative writing workshop, during personal introductions, and tell them I am schizophrenic without the entire class thinking, "He has said too much; it's amazing what people will tell a room full of strangers these days." We are taught to be ashamed; we are taught to keep our illness secret while moving through normie society. It's time for mental illness pride. It's time for us to stand up in front of a room full of strangers and say, "I'm schizophrenic; I am not ashamed."

Think of the times you have seen us, when you have seen those of us in the city who are homeless, talking angrily to ourselves because of psychosis, when you have seen those of us who walk through the city in dirty clothes and with eccentric mannerisms. These are only the most obvious of us; but there are many more who are better actors than these, and will never let you know they are sick. Do you think of these people as "others" as distinct from "people like us"? Do you think somehow that we suffer because of a sinful lifestyle, a weak mentality, laziness? I am here to tell you of our suffering, to tell you fully how it was manifested in one of us, and to say to you: Do not make us "others" anymore; make us your "people like us". I am proud to be schizophrenic, one of the one out of every hundred Americans who have the disease; and you would be fooling yourself if you thought, had it happened to you, you would have somehow taken control of it, and not let psychosis overtake your mental life. I know from experience there would have been no way for you to do so, had you really been stricken by schizophrenia.

39

Just after I had been discharged from my last long-term hospital, into a little room I rented in a one-story house with no central heat, one day I got to talking with a man about 6 or 7 years older than me at a bus stop. Somehow, I learned that he had schizophrenia, and I told him I too had it. We traded stories about our experiences with psychosis. (He told me of the time he stepped onto a plane to Japan and dropped something like three hits of acid just as the plane took off, which I knew would certainly lead to a psychotic agony the magnitude of which even I could not comprehend.)

I got the impression that his experiences with drugs had all taken place years ago, and that he still suffered from psychosis (he said he was on antipsychotic medication). Drugs seem to be merely the thing that kicks schizophrenia into action, but if it is truly schizophrenia, it will not go away even decades after one is clean, and most schizophrenics have never done drugs like LSD.

I had a good time talking with him, but at the time I had met many friends at the hospital, and was in no great need of companionship. He, on the other hand, seemed to lack friendship, and was quick to suggest we exchange numbers; such a chance meeting between two people with so much in common was rare. We exchanged numbers, and I soon forgot about it. Then, one day he called me, and wanted to meet with me somewhere for coffee. He needed friends, and I had seemed very much compatible with him. I told him something I still regret. I told him I didn't think it would be good for me, just then, to become friends with someone who had talked so much about drugs at the bus stop. I had only recently given up all drugs, and I didn't think such an association would be good for me. This was when I had plenty of healthy friends and associates from the hospital. This was before, one by one, they would all stop returning my calls, move on with their lives, and give up my friendship. I do not grudge them for it; that is how most friendships work, after all, as the years go by. But I did not make new friends, and I found that normies outside of hospital societies aren't as open to becoming friends with the mentally ill.

By the time I was that other schizophrenic's age, I was in much the same situation as he had been when I met him. I was lonely, I wanted a friend from whom I would not have to keep my illness secret, and to meet another schizophrenic at a bus stop, to share similar stories, would be a godsend to me. I regret what I said to him not so much because I believe we would somehow still be friends. I regret it more because, were another schizophrenic, whom I liked and who seemed to like me, to reject my friendship now, for such a silly reason as I'd had, I know how much of a hurtful disappointment it would be.

40

My father and stepmother are housesitting for my mother, who is out of town, so I'm spending some time with them at my mother's house. I spent last night here and I'll probably spend tonight here. Last night, my stepmother, Donna, told me she was reading a book my brother had given her by the radical Leftist Noam Chomsky. "Does David buy his stuff?" I said to my stepmother (David is my brother). "He bought it, but I don't know if he's read it," she said. "But does he buy it?" I said. "Yes," she said. "I told you he bought it." I knew she didn't understand my question, but I had a hard time putting it into other words. "Not the book," I said, "but does he buy it?" "Oh," she said, "I really don't know."

As I'm writing this, my father is taking the bread we have been baking out of the oven to check it. He's teaching me how to bake my own bread. I can just imagine myself, baking a loaf of bread every day at the cost of 40 or 50 cents, and eating it every night with dinner.

He told me Donna was going over to my part of town when I woke up this afternoon, and said she could drive me back to my place. He knows very well I still have to do my laundry. When I mentioned this to him he said, "Well, then, do you want to stay again tonight?" I told him I would. Now I'm obsessing on the thought that they had planned it this way, and Donna is over at my place now, going through all my personal things, to see if I have stolen anything from them. I don't like the thought of her going through all my things in my apartment. There's nothing I can do about it, after all, and no way for me to find out if she is.

41

I am still at my mom's with my father and stepmother. They are watching a film just behind me in the living room. I rarely watch films, and I almost never do with anyone else. I always stop the tape partway through several times when I watch videos, to take a break and do something else for an hour or two. It takes me usually two to four days to watch a movie. I will go to bed sometimes and wonder over what may happen by the end.

Tonight at dinner we were discussing environmental issues such as overpopulation. I was making a complex point about the economical impact of rising population. I was of the opinion that our economy, in order to grow, needs a certain magnitude of population growth. As I was making my point, Donna turned to my father and said, "Does that sound logical?" My father and stepmother will often pick apart my philosophical and political opinions to see if they are quite logical—to see whether they are only the results of psychosis. This has become more annoying lately. As I was making my point, suddenly I heard a sound that sounded like metal being struck very nearby—just outside the house in the direction of the garage. I paused, then heard it again. I said, "Did you hear that?" "No," they said; "hear what?" I was very embarrassed. I felt like I had to prove that I hadn't been hallucinating. There was no way I could do so. I listened again, and the noise didn't repeat itself. They hadn't heard it when it sounded the first two times. I said, frustrated, "It sounded like *boom boom*, just outside the garage." I realized there was no way to prove I hadn't been hallucinating, and now the point I was making was undermined by the suspicion that it was psychotic. I did not go back to it, but pretended to forget all about it.

42

With my delusional belief that everyone could hear my thoughts, during my first psychotic break, went a delusional belief that there was a rule, understood by everyone, that I must not tell anyone of my telepathy, discuss it overtly, or straight out ask anyone if he or she could hear my thoughts. I'm not sure where this came from. It may have been an extension of the "metaphorical speech" I perceived that night in the apartment with Al's friends. Just as with that speech that night with Al, Leo, and the others, there was an unspoken rule that one must never overtly state the implied meaning, so too now I believed there was such an unspoken rule, which everyone followed, that my thoughts were to be dealt with by others with only this sort of metaphorical speech. No one was to ask me overtly, "Why did you think of that sexual image just now?" just as I was not to ask anyone overtly, "Did you see that image that just passed through my mind?" Thus I was left to deal with these new powers alone, not expressing my anguish or emotions with speech, but only with my thoughts.

This psychosis was essentially a creative one. As I was sitting through class, or with my friends, or alone and communicating with that English teacher Lydia, in order not to only dwell on thoughts that anguished me, I would create visualization imagery shows to entertain people. This was sometimes purely an artistic endeavor: I was an artist whose medium was the mind's eye, and everything it was possible to imagine with it, and I would work and work, as everyone watched, at what sorts of images I could create. I created many images, that moved through time, that I considered masterpieces which I added to my portfolio, and would repeat for the enjoyment of whomever I was with. There were several such masterpieces I had that I recycled again and again, getting better and better at expressing the most I could with them; though I was constantly playing around with new images, looking for new masterpieces. At other times, such visualization was a means to symbolize my thoughts and what I was trying to communicate: the images would be a means of illustrating and simplifying my cognitive points by means of symbolism.

Such was the state I was in, in late October of 1989, when I was at my father's house alone, and my mother called. "Your father is here," she said to me, "and we have been discussing what would be best for you. We want you to see a therapist. I think you need perspective on your life."

"Yes," I thought, "perspective is precisely what I need." My emotion upon receiving this call was at once joyful and sad. I felt like crying. This call was like a sudden hope that I would not go on living forever as I was living: I would finally get "perspective"; I would finally find out from others, in a plain way, how my thoughts appeared to them, and figure out a way to solve the problem I had found myself in, the problem of this telepathy that had suddenly stricken me last summer.

I did not tell my mother these thoughts, or how I felt, with my voice, but only said, apathetically, "Okay. That's all? Bye, then."

43

My first meeting with my therapist didn't last long, according to my memory. All I remember of our interaction was that she asked me questions about my drug history, which I answered honestly, that I said to her, "I think people can hear my thoughts," and that she suggested hospitalization, and began to prepare me for what hospitalization would mean. She did not try to rationally convince me that people couldn't hear my thoughts. In fact, she seemed to take my statements to that effect as a matter of course, without asking me why I thought that, or trying to convince me otherwise, so that I took this as confirmation that people could hear my thoughts. She didn't tell me they could; but such a frank admission on her part, I thought, would be imprudent. Once I got confirmation, after all, there would be no way to get rid of my fear of humiliating thoughts, which even now plagued me every waking hour.

I remember that I told her the story of my first hospitalization. This had happened at the age of 15. I had been caught smoking pot by my mother, whose house I was living in at the time, and had been admitted to a drug rehabilitation hospital. I wasn't, at the time, ready to quit smoking pot and drinking; I just supposed every once in a while that I ought to cut down. I did not relate to all the addiction horror stories the other teenage addicts shared in that hospital. I made it clear that I was merely waiting until I was discharged so that I could go back to my former life. As a punishment for my non-cooperation, they made me stay in my room, alone, 24 hours a day, until I became ready to cooperate. I actually did not mind this; I sat by the window, looking out, all day long, feeling a romantic emotion of being a prisoner looking out upon freedom, and hoping one day to have it once more. I was not allowed any books. I did not mind that, either. I was perfectly happy to play the innocent, romanticized prisoner all day long, gazing out the window at his cherished, lost freedom.

One night, I picked a scab on the back of my neck. I had a lot of acne in that area back then, and this scab was infected. It started to bleed, so I put toilet paper over it to stop it; but no matter what I did, it continued to bleed. I went to the night nurse and told her. She said it would be very easy to stop the flow with a little ice. She took an ice cube, and pressed it into the small sore for a number of minutes. "Jason," she said, "what you're doing here is incredible to the staff. No one knows how to deal with it. They'll all be telling stories about you, a long time from now, a long time after you're gone."

After ten days of this, they discharged me. I was being kicked out.

I told this therapist now of this story, and I thought the hospital she was thinking of admitting me to would be similar. "I can always just get kicked out if I don't like it," I said. "They won't kick you out," she said, "no matter what you do."

I thought she only didn't understand my capability for non-cooperation, which had been inspired by the romanticized things I had learned of Gandhi and Martin Luther King. I thought if I simply refused to cooperate, at every level, for long enough, they would see that it would be no use to keep me there, and discharge me. But I had never been in a hospital such that she was suggesting I be admitted to. I would find that out soon enough.

44

Before I had gone to the therapist and to the hospital, there was a freshman student who attended my Western civilization history class, who sat right behind me. One day, he was gone. And several days after that he continued to be absent. Soon, somebody asked the teacher where this student, Daniel, was. "Daniel won't be joining us," the teacher replied. "I have a feeling he'll be gone for quite some time." When I got to the hospital, Bethesda Psychiatric, adolescent unit, I found out where Daniel had gone: he was a patient. He was there because of drug addiction, however, and wasn't there for the reasons I was. He took a leadership role in the drug treatment offered at that hospital, always claiming to be working through his issues and admitting his problem, always quick to jump on anything anyone said that was not quite addiction treatment standard.

In school he had been what you call a "stoner", coming up through the same social structures I had come up through, the social structures that produce workers for minimum wage restaurant, construction, carpet cleaning, and other unskilled jobs. He didn't care what having a good time and lagging behind in schoolwork would do to him later, any more than I did, or any of my friends. But he was a freshman that year, and I and all my friends were juniors; so we didn't really know each other.

At first, I took his attitude of completely tackling his drug addiction as sincere. But then, one day, I overheard one of the group leaders and a patient talking. "You do realize Daniel is just faking his way through this whole program, don't you?" said the patient. "Yeah," said the group leader; "everyone on staff knows he's not sincere, but that is how some addicts finally come to grips with their addiction, by pretending to so much they eventually start to believe it."

As for me, let's go back to the time right before I was admitted, that day I spent at home, knowing my parents and therapist had decided to hospitalize me. I had started this semester with a sit-down talk with my father, who laid out all our plans for how I would study, apply myself in school that year, and finally break out of the old patterns of apathy toward school, which had plagued me since the sixth grade. I really had a desire to change, too. When I would miss school after I started that junior year without an excuse from my parents, I would get detention. I thought detention was childish, so I didn't attend it. Then I would get suspended. I would go to school just as I did when I wasn't suspended, so that I could get all my work done, pass all the tests. Soon, the dean caught on that if he couldn't make me abide by suspension, the school would have no way to sanction my behavior. Suspension was the final consequence, which backed up the detention consequence; and if I didn't abide by it, why, this wouldn't be high school anymore, but college. So he alerted the police that often went through the school, and more often patrolled the parking lot and surrounding areas in their cars, to stop me if they saw me. If I was attending while suspended, I would be trespassing, and I would be arrested.

This digression is only meant to show that I was really dedicated, finally, to apply myself in school, that year which I had begun to attend during my first psychotic break. I was really trying, but I could never concentrate on anything; and my beginning algebra class was impossible for me. So though I was told by my parents that I needed not to attend school that day before I would be admitted to the hospital, I walked to school anyway in the afternoon, and turned in some papers I had due. As I was approaching the school, by means of a dirt path that connected the school parking lot to the 7-11 store and bowling alley where the students often went, I was filled with internal, stifled rage. I did not know why. I began to say angry things in my mind over and over; a thrash metal song went through my mind again and again, with the lyric, barked angrily, "Why am I always stuck for words!" I still do not quite understand that anger. Perhaps I was getting a clue, even then, of how much my life had been disrupted, of all I had lost, and of just what kind of struggle was just beginning.

45

By the time I was to be dropped off at and admitted to the hospital by my father, I was looking forward to it. I still had very little idea of just where I was going. Perhaps I would be going to a place with other telepaths like myself, a place where we were taught how to use and control our powers. Perhaps, finally, I would end up working for the government, using my telepathic powers for espionage or intelligence. On the other hand, perhaps I was merely going to a place where I could stop doing drugs, discipline my mind, get involved in transcendental meditation, explore my miraculous powers, become enlightened, finally to end up as a powerful yogi able to communicate with my mind without any fear of humiliation. I was looking forward to finally working on the problem, and solving it. Then, maybe I would return to Lydia after six months or a year, having disciplined and learned to control my mind, and sweep her off her feet. "Certainly my powers are important and I ought to cherish them," I said to myself; "this pain they give me is only the natural result of their being so powerful, and of my discovering them so suddenly. But I have many years ahead of me to explore, develop, and discipline my mind."

On the way to the hospital, my father and I went to a three-story bookstore in Cherry Creek, the Tattered Cover, and I picked up five or six New Age books on shamanism and transcendental meditation. These I was going to read as a part of learning this mental discipline that would be the key to controlling, and developing, my telepathy. Often, when I had been particularly disturbed by humiliating thoughts, I had sent thoughts to people that said, "But all of this isn't the least important compared to the importance of my powers—this is all childish nonsense compared to the very phenomenon by which I was humiliated." I had this sense then. The world, and the rest of my life, lay open before me: there were so many possibilities for the future, and though I was in agony because of my powers now, I was, after all, only 17, and I had only discovered these powers a few months earlier. Certainly with the help of the people where I was that very night going away to, certainly once my telepathy was tested and confirmed, certainly in an environment where sympathetic people could overtly discuss my telepathy with me, only great things could happen, and I could only have a life of greatness ahead of me.

46

I've been thinking this morning about the nature of belief. What is a belief?

I have a thought, right now, that the abandoned Volkswagen Van in front of my house, that has been there for perhaps six months, has machinery inside of it that allows the government to monitor me from another location. This thought says that it transmits the contents of my computer, as I surf the web or write, to the government, the FBI. I do not believe this thought: it is only a thought I have. At what point, then, does that thought become a belief? I already think about it a lot. I do not consider that I believe it. What makes a thought a belief?

Belief is a mysterious thing—we take it for granted that it is very clear what constitutes a belief, but for one whose entire belief system can change in a matter of days, it becomes very shadowy and difficult to define. Sometimes, when I have been thinking paranoid thoughts, I have asked myself, "Do I really believe these thoughts?" And then I have answered, "I do not know if I believe them—I do not know even what belief is at all."

47

When I was in the sixth grade, in elementary school, getting a girl-friend was as simple as walking up to a girl you knew and saying, "Will you go with me?" If she said, "Yes," you were boyfriend and girlfriend: you would do things together after school, you would spend time together at recess, you might hold hands or kiss. There was one girl I particularly liked that year, but I was painfully ashamed at liking her, and afraid my friends would find out. She was in many of my classes, and had a kind of down-to-earth, even uncouth charm about her (she wore usually simple clothes that were not stylish, jeans and shirts, and a tattered green Army coat). I would talk to her and play with her at recess as she gradually became one of my group of friends. One day, I walked up to her and said, "Will you go with me?" I had finally decided that there was nothing to be ashamed of in liking a girl, that this was something the others took as a matter of course. "Yes," she said.

But our relationship didn't last long. I was still ashamed of liking her. I was ashamed to spend time with her after school, hold her hand, or put my arm around her. One day, on a day that really wasn't that chilly, we were walking back in from recess, and she said, "I'm cold." One of my friends told me this was a hint that I should put my arm around her. But I was too ashamed to do so. I wanted to, and yet I was afraid to.

I remember my thoughts about this later that day. To put my arm around her was putting "weight" on reality—the reality in which I had really asked her, "Will you go with me?" in which she had really said, "Yes," and in which I was really her boyfriend. I theorized that such reality could change at any moment, just as it is possible for me to see something completely different, and be in completely different surroundings, five minutes from now. My whole reality could change—I thought it was possible—so that if I put my arm around her or kissed her, suddenly she would be a complete stranger, who wasn't my girlfriend, who knew nothing of me. Such an act would be rendered completely inappropriate. I was afraid that, if I put "weight" on reality, just as one rests one's body weight on a bridge, by trusting that reality wouldn't change, by trusting that she really was my girlfriend, it could suddenly break beneath me. I saw the possibility of reality suddenly becoming completely altered in the next moment, and so I dreaded doing anything that trusted too completely the present reality, the reality I had come to know, in which she really wanted me to put my arm around her. By junior high school, I remember continuing to muse on this theory, walking through the halls and imagining that reality was a tattered bridge that could break at any moment; and so I said to myself, "Take care not to put very much weight on that bridge, as do the fools all around you. It could break and leave you helpless at any moment, so do not do anything that trusts too completely in the reality you have come to know."

48

What is going through my mind today? What has been going on inside of me, as I sit with the radio on, thinking and thinking, cup of tea by cup of tea, cigarette by cigarette?

Let's see…how did this start? Oh yes: I was thinking of what may happen to me if I ever become the glorified, recognized artist I am always projecting that I will be in the future. Bear with me if this sounds self-glorifying, but I have had, for years, a notion in the back of my mind of myself as: JSR, Great Writer, Tragically Penniless, Genius Artist. Since I (even against my will) have this silly notion firmly embedded in my mind, it's hard to write a memoir that doesn't somehow involve it.

What problems did I foresee in this future? I foresaw controversy. The controversy will focus on my acquaintances from my past (I have very few present acquaintances).

First off: Al, whom I mentioned earlier. Though some of my other friends talked about and fantasized about crime, Al was the only one who was really criminal. In that fall of 1989, when I was still bewildered by psychosis, one day he showed up at my father's house, and said he knew where there was a car with the keys in it, in an unlocked garage. He rattled off the make and model (which I have forgotten), and regarded this as a special opportunity. "I'm not touching it," I said to him. What was I going to do with a car? I didn't need a car, and was in no especial need of money. "Just go out there with me," said Al. "All you have to do is stand there."

I didn't, at the time, know why he wanted me to stand there as he stole the car. When I would later tell this story to a judge, in Santa Monica, as a reason why I shouldn't be a juror on a car theft trial, the judge's probing questions made it clear to me. Al was worried that the owner of the car would come out as he was stealing it, and wanted someone there to back him up. I had actually helped him steal it.

But this all seemed harmless enough at the time. All I had to do was stand just outside the garage. I went out there and watched him steal the car, then went back home and forgot all about it. Al was arrested joyriding in the car that weekend, and spent the next few months in prison. I was never implicated in anything. According to me, I still hadn't done anything wrong; I still didn't know why Al had wanted me to stand there, and I thought to myself, "He was the one who stole the car—I didn't do it after all." When I was in my second hospital, over a year later, I learned that Al was in prison again for shooting someone at a party.

But this wasn't the controversy that worried me so much.

It was another acquaintance I had, a good friend in Los Angeles I will call Marty, who I always suspected was a rapist, in a paranoid way, without any direct evidence. This man was my roommate for a few years, who was a very angry person. We got into verbal arguments quite a bit, and he was very difficult to deal with, though at other times we got along, and I still consider him a friend, though one I have lost contact with. But when I overheard someone from a neighboring building tell the apartment manager that there had been some attempted rapes in our alley, I immediately suspected him, though I did not have any evidence, and this was only paranoia on my part. I even thought he was running to another state from the law, one weekend when he, all of a sudden, took off to visit Disneyland, and stayed there several nights. I was sure at the time the police would break down my door, at any second, with a warrant for his arrest; but this did not happen. He merely came back from Disneyland when his weekend was over, even with videotape of all the things he had seen there.

But as I was thinking today, thinking too much as I am prone, I began to suspect, even to believe that he had committed murders while living in my very apartment. He had done it during the times when he was away on vacation. He had never been caught, until perhaps in these past few years when I would know nothing of it, and now he was either on the lam or in prison.

About a year ago I saw a man on a bicycle across the street from me as I was walking home. It was a narrow, busy street. This man looked just like Marty. He was riding a bicycle just as Marty used to do, with those headphones on that he always listened to music with while riding (Marty never had a car, and got around town on his bicycle). He looked just like him: he had that same cap to cover his balding head that worried him so much, the same jet-black hair below it, the same thin, pale face, the same shadow of stubble that even darkened his face right after he would shave. I stared at him, he stared at me, and I began to become convinced that it was he. I made a move to cross the street, and he took off down the street on his bike. But Marty didn't live in Denver: he lived in West LA. I called his old number that day. It was disconnected. I called his sister, who was also a good friend of mine, and she told me, no, he still lived in LA and was there now, and she gave me the same disconnected number I already had for him. He often didn't pay his phone bill on time, and only paid it later once it was disconnected and he had to pay a massive reconnection fee and deposit, so it was likely this had happened. I kind of put it out of my mind and forgot about it.

But just today I was thinking, "What if that really was he, what if he had been running from the law, and his sister had only been covering for him? He certainly knows if I were to find out he had done something, I would turn him in. What if he were running for something he had done even while living with me?" This went on and on, until the police had been for years tapping my phone in case he called, and were monitoring me this very moment from that Volkswagen Van that still sits abandoned in front of the my building.

I have tried his number again, and all I get is a woman answering, *"¿Buenas noches?"* with the warm sounds of young, boisterous children in the background. It has been a good four years since I have spoken to him.

This is where the irony starts to creep in. I have been afraid, as I write this, and still am, that all this really is true. And if I publish this, it will be perceived by the police as a frank admission that I knew of his crimes in LA, and I will be charged with harboring him since I didn't turn him in at the time. Why, then, do I write this? Part of me knows the paranoia of my mind, the way it gets me to fear the police and FBI and law, the way it makes me think they are just looking for an excuse to lock me up. The way it creates these conceptual frameworks with which I explain this feeling I have that they are tapping my phone and bugging my apartment. The way, in short, that it has fooled me time and time again. I write this, looking at the words, knowing they sound paranoid, trying to be as non-psychotic as I can in this narrative (I don't like the idea of playing the unreliable narrator without my design), and I say to myself, "It is only fantasy." And then there is this fear in my gut: "No, it's all true, and you'll go to prison if you publish this."

Before writing this (here comes into the picture that ridiculous, almost comic image, JSR: Famous Writer With Romanticized Tragic Past), I only thought that in this future glory that will one day be mine, I would be the subject of tabloid headlines, due to my friendship with Marty, which will be discovered from this narrative. Now, I think the tabloids will read that I actually knew of Marty's crimes, and did nothing about it, because of this chapter. Worse than that, I will be indited and thrown into prison, with this very chapter as evidence.

It is a fear I have right now, which I may not have tomorrow. Just as in elementary and junior high school, I feared putting too much weight on reality; now I have learned, over the years of being psychotic, not to put weight on paranoid beliefs, not to act as if they were true. No matter how strong the belief is, if I can say to myself, "Would my psychiatrist call this paranoia?" and answer, "Yes," I will not act on these beliefs. Or, in the present chapter, I will positively act as if they weren't true, in a way that could be disaster if they were.

If you are reading this, you know that my fear of the police did not overcome me, and I have not deleted this chapter. One more point for reason over paranoia. Or am I only going through the motions, as I have been taught to do in this world, believing one thing, and acting on beliefs that contradict it, the beliefs the normie mind takes as reality? It has been a contradictory and absurd life of mine, constantly living in one belief system, and always acting, as much as I can, as if it were all false. It is no wonder schizophrenics become apathetic to everything, being taught as they are to act as if all their beliefs weren't true, and to act upon ideas they hold to be false.

49

When I was admitted to the hospital, at first I was shown into a clean, comfortable room with two beds, and a bathroom just around the corner. There was a nightstand with a set of drawers, florescent lights I could turn on and off as I pleased, a high ceiling, a Plexiglas window, and plenty of space. Just when I had situated myself in this room, and met my roommate, I was told: no, I would have to stay in a different room. Then, I was shown into a room that I would later learn the other patients called "the fishbowl". It was small—just a bed, a hard tile floor, and an overhead light. But there was something more. The wall at the head of the bed—that entire wall—was a window, behind which the people in the nurse's station went about their business. Through this window, they could look in at any time (and they did) to make sure I was all right, to "monitor" me. I didn't want to stay in this room, and I told them so. My therapist soon showed up with the nurse who had shown me this room, and the nurse explained that they would have to monitor closely anyone who had been "seeing" things constantly, as I had told my therapist I had been. She had taken what I had said about my creative visualizations, and thought they were hallucinations. I didn't quite have the capacity, at the time, to point out the difference. Yes: I "saw" my creative visualizations in the sense that I could tell you in detail all about them and how they looked; I just didn't see them with my eyes. I wasn't sure how to explain this distinction.

Soon, I was given my classical guitar. I had played guitar since I was about 12, played both classical and rock music. For a while I and my friends had a band, but the band broke up when the other band members (whom I wasn't with at the time) broke into the drummer's house, and stole some things. The drummer was a good friend of mine, and while he broke off contact with our little clique at the time, I stayed in contact with both him and the other band members. In any case, that was the end of the band; so I had given up on rock music, and studied only classical, with private lessons.

I began to play my classical guitar, sitting on the edge of the bed, and played for perhaps a half-hour. This had often delighted me when I was in the grip of the deepest psychosis. Once, after school not long before, I had played a minuet by Bach for my friend Frederick as we sat in my father's living room. During the song, I made one set of notes stand for my romantic overture to Lydia, the next set her apprehensive reply; and thus the dialogue went on between us, until in the end she went along with my romantic wishes, and the dialogue became a song sung in unison, proclaiming our happiness together. As I had been playing, I had been visualizing Lydia sitting across from me; I believed not only that Frederick saw her too, but that she, wherever she was, could hear my music in her mind. When the minuet was over, Frederick said to me, "Someone was here. Your bitch." I did not take offense at his calling Lydia a bitch; this was how we all referred to one another's girlfriends. He was telling me: I saw here sitting here, listening to your song: you certainly brought her here with your mind, and she was listening too.

But after I had played for a half-hour or so, one of the staff came in and told me it was time to give my guitar back, as I would have to go to bed, and wouldn't be allowed to keep it with me. "No," I said. "You can't keep it with you," he said; "it's dangerous." "Let me put it this way," I said: "unless you are insane enough to get violent over this, the guitar is staying with me tonight."

According to procedure, they ought to have gotten violent over this. I would learn this soon enough. But perhaps because of the counsel of my therapist (I suspect this was the reason), they decided not to give me such a rude awakening my first night there.

He left, very flustered, after I said this to him, then came back a few minutes later. "We've talked about it," he said, "and we think the guitar is good for you, to ease your mind. We'll let you keep it for now."

50

One thing that was a very hard lesson for me, especially once I was admitted to my second adolescent hospital, Cleo Wallace in Westminster, Colorado, was that Gandhi's philosophy of non-cooperation simply does not work when dealing with (what I thought was) oppression by mental health professionals. If you don't cooperate, and force them to take you down, they will only cheapen your noble non-cooperation by calling it "passive-aggressive behavior", and this will be seen as a symptom of mental illness, and a sign that you cannot be released. You will be punished more, physically and psychologically, until you give up this "passive-aggressive" behavior; and they, after all, lose nothing by being forced to punish you or take you down, and you lose everything. On the other hand, that other type of resistance that Gandhi shunned, violent resistance, works even less. At Cleo Wallace, if you landed a swing at a staff member during a physical takedown, they called the police, and filed assault charges which you will no doubt be convicted of; and with enough convictions they transfer you to jail. When you get out of jail, where do you go? Usually back to Cleo Wallace. This was not the type of resistance I gave them. I chose the good old, saintly, noble-oppressed-young-man-being-subject-to-unjust-oppression-and-responding-only-with-justice, great as Gandhi, non-cooperation.

At this second institution I was in, Cleo Wallace, once physical non-cooperation only resulted in painful takedowns and a transferal to the lockdown unit, I decided on a hunger strike. I refused my dinner and the next day threw my breakfast into the trash. Certainly they would ask me why I did this. They did not. They did not even seem to notice. I threw away my lunch when that came. They still did not ask me why. This went on for over 50 hours, by which time I was famished. When my dinner came, I finally ate it. I never even got the opportunity to declare my hunger strike. I thought, "Had I been Gandhi and gone on with it, they would have only buried me after I starved, and forgotten all about it." I concluded, "This is not at all like those history books make fighting oppression out to be; they seem to say it is so simple, while this is so very frustrating and absurd." I had been very gullible in grade school.

51

The next day, my second day in Bethesda Psychiatric, one of the group leaders, Anne, asked me what was going on in my mind. We were not in a therapy group, but sitting alone in the dayroom after one. She was a thin, tall woman in her forties, who wore long skirts from which she was constantly picking off single, stray, long red hairs that had originated on her head. She had a very warm face and smile, the kind of expression that you feel like you can trust, and tell her anything. "I think people can hear my thoughts," I said. She did not contradict me.

52

The first person to tell me he could not hear my thoughts was, strangely, my insurance case manager. I was on my father's insurance, and this illness of mine, if it turned out to be schizophrenia, as the staff suspected, could end up being quite costly to my insurance company. So early on in my hospitalization, he came and met with me, something the staff and my therapist were very offended by; but they could not stop him. I had an interview with him in a small office room which he began by asking, "You say you think people can hear your thoughts?" I did not, at the time, know who this person was or why it was important to tell him the truth. I had held my silence about my delusion so long, it was difficult for me to tell its contents to people; it seemed like a private, personal thing. This was probably why the staff thought the interview wasn't a good idea. But I did not lie to him: I answered his questions honestly, which was a difficult, and a lucky thing. When I told him Yes, I thought people could hear my thoughts, he said to me very clearly, "Well I just want you to know that I can't hear your thoughts," and then went on with his questions. He was the first to contradict my psychotic beliefs; but this did not convince me people couldn't hear my thoughts: I went right back to playing my creative visualization picture shows, and trying vainly to avoid humiliating thoughts, within seconds. Perhaps this was why Anne didn't bother with contradicting me.

53

Another memory I have of my early days at that hospital was when I was in a group, and we were discussing LSD. "How often were you taking LSD?" asked the group leader of me. I did not know him, but my sentiments were not particularly fond of him. "About once every month or two," I said. He burst out laughing and said, "You expect me to believe that? Really, tell the truth." I grew angry and said, "That is the truth!" He immediately saw that my appearance signified more than mere LSD burnout, and said sheepishly, "Oh," then went on to other things.

54

I understand now why he had thought I was an acidhead who tripped two or three times a week, as some students in my high school did. Once I was on medication and had left this delusion behind, one day my therapist said to me, "You look a lot better." "How did I look before?" I asked. Her eyes widened as if she were struggling to put my former appearance into words. "You looked like you were walking through a fog," she said.

55

I do not know when my last shower was. Sometime shorter than nine days ago, but longer than six. My father has read part of this manuscript already. "I go days without a shower too," he said. "Why do you do it?" I said. "When you don't automatically shower every day as a matter of course," he said, "you kind of aren't exactly sure when you should shower." Maybe that's my problem. But I really should brush my teeth more.

Today I went shopping for flour, sugar, yeast, and eggs, so that I can make my own bread. I didn't want to brush my hair, so I just put a knit cap on. I wore jeans that had powdered sugar stuck in their fabric from the small gem doughnuts I had eaten in the morning. I wore a shirt that had two large, round olive oil stains on their front. Put a tweed jacket on, and I was ready to go. But one more thing: I slipped on my empty camping backpack in which to carry back the groceries.

As I was walking to the store, I kept smelling armpit musk, and I wondered for a second where it was coming from, until I realized I was the only one around.

If someone were to ask me, "Don't you care what the people in the store think of you?" I would say, "No, not in the least." I am not there to pick up on women; I am not there to make friends with anybody; what is it to me if the other shoppers and employees have a low opinion of me? Besides, there are enough people like me in that neighborhood so that I won't stand out. In Los Angeles, the poor are mostly blacks and immigrants. Here in Denver, at least in my neighborhood, almost all the homeless I see are whites who dress similar to me. Supposing someone takes me for one of them? Does this matter? It may to my mother, but it doesn't matter in the least to me.

But let me get back to the point I was making. There was a man at the checkout line, buying only salsa and tortillas, which he held in his hands instead of in a handheld cart. He had on mud-stained work boots and his jeans below the knee had splashes of mud. He looked somewhat Caucasian in his features, but had dark skin and straight, jet-black hair under his baseball cap. On his upper lip was a mustache whose hairs were black and trimmed short. He immediately struck me as an undercover INS agent. If you could imagine a middle-class American with dark skin, who doesn't speak a word of Spanish, and works as a gym teacher or car salesman, dressed up like a working-class Mexican, this was precisely how this man's expression, and how he carried himself, appeared. But he was obviously playing the part of a Mexican. Why? Well, he must be an INS agent, there to get people to admit where they're from, then flash his INS id, and ask them for their immigration paperwork.

But was he after me? He did, after all, take a long glance at me as he was leaving.

Once, last summer, I was sitting out on my front porch with the old widow from downstairs, when a Latino immigrant walked by. He stopped and tried to pick a plum from my next-door neighbor's plum tree. I didn't notice he was there until the old widow said, "Shake it!" meaning he should shake the tree. When he looked at her, slightly abashed, and continued walking by, I said, *"¿De donde eres?"* "Guatemala," he said. *"Mi padre ha ido a Guatemala,"* I said, and we conversed for about ten minutes. The widow asked me to translate several things to him, then disappeared suddenly and came back with a plastic cup of ice water for him (it was very hot out).

A few days later, the old widow said to me, "Are you an illegal immigrant?" "No," I said, "I was born in California." "Well if you are," she said, "you certainly did a good job of getting rid of your accent." Just last December, she left a paper for me in the hallway, with a front-page article on a possible amnesty for Mexican undocumented immigrants. The words, *Undocumented aliens may get amnesty,* were underlined in pen.

Perhaps she tipped off the INS about me, then. Well, I thought, if she did, and they deported me, think of what a black eye it would be for the INS.

But I don't want to think about all that anymore. Thinking about it has exhausted me. I can't help it, but I'll try to put it down. For now, it's time for a shower.

56

One night, after I had been at Bethesda perhaps a week, and was still psychotic and refusing medication, my father showed up to take me home. He wasn't willing to accept what the doctors there had told him—that I may have schizophrenia, that I may need long-term treatment, lasting perhaps the rest of my life. As for me, I didn't know what a schizophrenia diagnosis might mean; I was too psychotic to have any conception of all I would lose with that diagnosis. But my father perfectly understood all he had lost with it—and he wasn't yet willing to accept it. One of the staff showed me in to my father in the atrium. We sat down and the staff member said, "Now Jason, tell your father what you've been telling us—it's important that you be honest." "I think people can hear my thoughts," I said. "When did you start thinking that?" said my father. "After you were admitted here?" "A few months ago," I said. "Before." "Why does that bother you?" said my father. "What's wrong with people hearing your thoughts? How do they know the thoughts came from you?" One way or another, during our conversation, my father changed his mind about taking me home. He became convinced that I really needed to be there, that I wasn't only being psychologically manipulated by the therapists and doctors.

He knew he couldn't afford to completely support me the rest of my life, and he was worried about my future—how would I work?—what sort of life lay ahead of me?—would I be homeless? At another time early on, he came to my room and told me I shouldn't worry about how I would make a living, that he had learned of a government program that supports the disabled, which I would probably qualify for. But I hadn't been worried about my future in the least. He was the one who was consumed by such worry.

He felt like he had lost his son. I wanted to say to him, "Here I am, I am the same person," but I was not the same person, and he would have to learn to accept a new, different son, if he wanted his son back. He eventually did.

57

My father wasn't the only one who feared psychological manipulation at the hospital. Ever since my first night there, when I had heard the nurse's announcement: "Medication!" and had seen all the patients line up at the medication window, one by one being handed a tiny paper cup of pills, and a tiny paper cup of water, I had been suspicious of medication. It had seemed to me only a means of psychological control—something that conditioned us to be obedient and turned us into God knew what…turned us into mental patients. This was why I refused it. I had gone without medication all my life…I had only run into mental problems when I discovered my telepathy, and so I was there to discipline and control my telepathy. Medication was completely irrelevant.

But after I had been there eight or ten days, and had been taken down physically and put into seclusion for two or three days (the story I mentioned in the beginning), I completely changed my mind. My first day of seclusion, my therapist came in to see me. She was horrified at what had happened to me. She could see clearly—as so many in the mental health community and even the general public do not see—that schizophrenics did nothing wrong to become sick, and so giving them physical punishment for being sick only causes them to suffer more. They do not deserve such punishment, or deserve to be locked up, any more than your average Joe on the street; they never asked to be sick, after all. She probably saw also that my disobedient temperament was doing me disservice—and probably would continue to—in the world of psychological treatment. She asked me again to take the medication. I had been beaten and humbled, and I wanted all this trouble to end. If she thought the medication could help me, I became suddenly willing to try it.

That wasn't the last time I would have to be taken down and put into seclusion at that hospital, though. Though takedowns can be very painful—the way all the hands grab at you and twist your limbs around into helpless positions, the way one man will lie across your back, pressing your chest into the floor, the rug burns and floor scrapes—at least one other time I remember growing frustrated at being so controlled, and forcing a takedown. This time, however, I knew it was coming. As soon as I saw that it was about to take place, instead of complying and walking to seclusion, I ran into my bathroom, and began to wet my arms and ankles. When they all came into my room and went after me, I gave them quite a wrestling match. A week later, when I was out of seclusion and back in my room, I was eating with a new patient and one of the male staff who had taken me down. "If they ever have to take me down," said the new patient, a male, "they'll have a real hard time of it, I can tell you that." "What makes you think we didn't have a hard time of it with Jason?" said the staff member.

58

I just got done with having dinner at my mother's with my father, stepmother, my childhood friend Joe, and his wife Sarah, who is also my pharmacist. At one point Joe said to me, "You look like you've lost weight." "It's the Loxapine," I said. "You mean it's working better for you?" said Sarah. "I mean it gives me less appetite," I said. "When I was on Haldol I had a much larger appetite." "That's one thing they say about Haldol," said Sarah. "There's a newer one, Zyprexa, that's also supposed to give you less appetite."

I really like Joe and Sarah. Whenever I am with them, it is as little uncomfortable to discuss my mental illness or medication as it would be discussing medication for high cholesterol or diabetes. It is not so comfortable with others. I suppose my mother's friends know I have schizophrenia, though I have never told them; I'm sure my mother has. But eating dinners with them, if the subject gets too close to mental illness, it is quickly steered away, as if mental illness is some sort of skeleton in our family closet.

I have a feeling it would be like this if I attended the dinners my father and stepmother have been putting together for friends of theirs who are strangers to me. If they don't know I'm schizophrenic, they would ask the simple questions that always fluster me like, "So what do you do?" or, "Why did you move back from LA?" And even if they know I'm schizophrenic I would be just as uncomfortable, because that's how I am with strangers, especially strangers of the middle-class such that all my parents' friends are. Though I grew up middle-class, I find that as the years go by, and I have had none of the experiences of that class—such as working a steady job, owning a house, finding a stable mate, etc.—I have a very hard time relating socially to those people. Not only do I not fit in, but I do not particularly like them. They are always making witty little remarks and they seem to have had a good time only when they have made enough of them to have made a good impression on the others.

But in any case, I found going over our experiences in youth with Joe very interesting tonight, and I did not particularly feel any shame in openly discussing my medication—even using that dreaded word "antipsychotic" medication. This is how it ought to be at every dinner—even one with strangers. We take it as such a matter of course that mental illness is a subject of shame, that we do not always see anything wrong with the fact that discussing it or admitting it openly in social situations makes people so uncomfortable. It is really a disease like any other—like cancer, clogged arteries, diabetes, arthritis. Mentally ill people did not do anything wrong to become mentally ill—it just happened to them, like heart attacks happen. Can you imagine what it would be like, if after ever having a heart attack and being in the hospital, one had to lie to strangers about it, keep it secret from bosses and professors, and keep clear from openly discussing it at dinners with people who know about it? But if anyone ever has a schizophrenic episode, and a stay in a mental ward, even if that person gets completely better, he or she will keep it secret from dates, employers, and acquaintances, as if it is some skeleton in one's closet, like being arrested for domestic abuse. We suffer enough from our illness; this is bad enough; it only makes it worse when the very fact of our having it becomes a social taboo.

59

Before going on medication at Bethesda, after I was let out of "the fishbowl" and allowed into an ordinary room with a roommate, I had a roommate (whose name I have forgotten) whom I will call Will. Will was an ordinary kid, I think about 18 years old, who had attempted suicide. His main reason for attempting suicide, as far as I could tell from our conversations, had to do with a relationship with a young woman he had been involved in, and which I think had ended just before the suicide attempt. He would talk on and on at night, as I displayed my creative visualization picture shows for him, and from what I could tell from what he was saying, he was planning on attempting suicide again, and succeeding this time. It seemed very clear to me that this was what he was suggesting.

Will had a little CD player with headphones, and often played for me the gentle, relaxing New Age music he loved so much. I had been listening only to the harsh, though melodic, sounds of my thrash metal, punk, and industrial music up to that point, so this New Age piano, synthesizer, and drum machine music, that seemed so gentle and pleasing, was a new pleasure to me. I ended up buying several such CDs over the next few years of this semi-psychedelic, relaxing New Age stuff, which gave me peace and infinite pleasure even when imprisoned indefinitely in institutions.

I thought I ought to say something to the staff about his plan for suicide, and so I did. I privately pulled a male group leader aside, whom I had come to trust, and told him that Will was planning on suicide as soon as he got out. "What exactly did he say?" asked the group leader. I grew kind of flustered. I realized then that the meaning I had perceived in Will's language had not been straightforward and clear. "It just seems like he's suggesting it," I said. "But what did he say?" said the staff member. I did not really remember what Will had said—the exact words he had used—I only remembered this "sense" of meaning I got, in whose terms everything he said could be easily understood. "It wasn't exactly what he said," I told the group leader, "he was just suggesting it, not saying it precisely." I had a very difficult time finding the words to describe how I got this "sense" of meaning, that seemed so natural and real to me, and yet could not exactly be found in any one sentence Will had said that I could repeat.

The group leader spoke with Will alone, and Will did not upbraid me or say anything about it to me at all, though he was to be discharged soon, and such an accusation could cause him to have to stay there a good time longer. Soon, he was discharged, and I never found out if he ever repeated his suicide attempt, or heard anything about him ever again.

60

I have only good memories of Bethesda Psychiatric after I went on medication. They put me on a good dose of Stelazine while I was still in seclusion, as soon as I had agreed to take it; and from then on, things got better. I simply forgot I was a telepath. It wasn't like I became convinced finally that I had no telepathic powers; it was just that I wasn't interested in it very much anymore, so that even if I were to make an effort to send thoughts to people, I found it difficult, and grew bored with it. Though I had trouble explaining certain things people had said a month before which seemed to match perfectly my thoughts, I began to feel like an idiot for ever having believed I was a telepath. One day, at lunch, I was eating with my therapist, and she asked me did I feel different than before, as I certainly looked better.

"I'm embarrassed," I said. "Why?" she said. "I'm embarrassed that I believed in all that before," I said. She became her normal over-sympathetic, almost maternal self, and said, "Oh, no, that's nothing to be embarrassed about! Nothing at all!"

At each meeting in which we all introduced ourselves, one-by-one, to a new patient, we all gave our reason for being there. My reason, as I was taught to say by my therapist, was "thought disorder". A schizophrenia diagnosis is only made after the symptoms persist for at least six months, so my status thus far was provisional. So far as I could tell from all these introductions, I was the only schizophrenic there. No one else was there for psychosis or "thought disorder" or schizophrenia, but most people were there for delinquency, drug use, maladjustment, suicidal ideation, child abuse issues, etc. I have only been to two hospitals that primarily treated mental illnesses such as schizophrenia and bipolar disorder, and both of them after I was off my father's insurance and onto state insurance (the last, the county hospital here in Denver, I was only at for one night).

Bethesda, however, with its emphasis on therapy and the fact that they weren't there merely to punish you for every little thing, was a good place for me. There was no one who was generally disliked, but we were all accepting of any other patient, no matter how different, and everyone got a sense of being in a very supportive community. All group therapy is really is conversation, guided and directed by a leader; and so we had our laughs, our deep moments, our light moments, our tears. It was a place where you automatically had friends, and got to know everyone else on a very personal level. Though I myself had difficulty interacting with people, with my apathetic nature and dazed out mentality from the medication, I at least felt like everyone liked me; and I certainly liked everyone else.

Christmas passed by this way, and into the new year, 1990. My discharge date rolled around, and preparations were beginning to be made for my release.

61

I do not know how many times I have taken LSD. I would say a good estimate is anywhere between 12 and 16 times. Certainly this has done some damage; but I have known people who took it two or three times a week for their entire junior or senior high school year, and into their 20s they appeared completely normal, with no noticeable mental problems.

The memories of the last two times I took it. They were both at institutions. I smuggled some into the residential unit of Cleo Wallace Center in the summer of 1990 after a home pass the second to last time I took it. The last time was in January of 1991 in the lockdown unit, when someone smuggled it in to me.

That time, the LSD wasn't very strong, and I only took one hit. My best friend in the hospital at that time was named Mark. I first met Mark when I was transferred to the lockdown unit, and found myself eating at his table with some others. "Do you know Jason Ratcliff?" said Mark. "I am Jason Ratcliff," I said. Apparently, Mark had been told to ask about me by my friend on the outside, Pat. I had sold Pat my amplifier for about $150, and told him he could pay me later back in June of 1989. The amplifier was then stolen from Pat, and he never paid me; I don't think he had the money anyway. But I had forgiven him, and Mark and I became good friends—we had friendship with Pat in common, as well as many other things. Mark had a way of making a joke of some commonplace phrase or silly little sentence, so that I could not control my laughs. "Everyone likes to drink...WATER. I certainly do like...WATER. There's nothing so good as some good...WATER," he would say, and go on and on with this silliness, until I was splitting my sides with laughter.

Anyway, in January of 1991 Mark came back from a pass and handed me a hit of acid. "I thought you'd enjoy it," he said.

The acid tab was still under my lip when I had to take my medication. They made you open your mouth to make sure you swallowed the pills, so when I did so I tried to keep the acid tab under my lip. The nurse looked at me suspiciously and asked me to open my mouth again. I did so. "Okay," she said after a look. No problem.

For some reason, I decided to go to bed early. I didn't have a roommate at the time, and the door was ajar. My door faced another door to a room that was unoccupied at the time, and to the left of it was a bathroom, to the right, through a threshold that had no door, was the dayroom. The other patients were watching TV and playing board games and chatting. The sounds of their chatter came into my room. The light of the dayroom streamed through my slightly open door. I still had not noticed any effects of the LSD. It had been over an hour since I had finally swallowed the piece of blotter. Perhaps my high dose of medication was keeping me sane. But I was not quite sane. I was aroused.

My erection pushed up through my underwear and would not be ignored. I began to give it satisfaction. Now, I think I felt the LSD, just a little bit. Only in the morning did I realize that I had masturbated with the door ajar, around the corner from which people were going about their business, watching TV, laughing, eating snacks. If anyone had heard noises, he or she did not say anything about it to me the next day. I cannot imagine that they didn't hear it, though.

62

I almost always enjoyed LSD when I took it, no matter how psychotic it made me. That was why, as recently as 1995, when I thought I was taking it, I went ahead. Thought I was taking it? Let me explain.

I was going to Santa Monica College at the time. There was a young woman in my geology class who took a special interest in me, and I thought, due to a complex paranoid delusion, that she was working according to the wishes of certain other professors who had it in for me. She was there to get evidence against me of plagiarism, to get me to sleep with her illegally (was she really 20, as she said, or only 17?), or she was there to get me to take LSD and end up in a mental ward. One day, I showed up to school with my own semen dried up in a large stain just at the ankle of my jeans. I didn't notice it till later, but I'm sure others did. If she noticed it, she didn't seem to take offense, but came up to me from behind, and put her arms over my shoulders and hugged me. I wasn't sure how to respond, so I didn't.

But at another time, she was drinking from a bottle of water, and said to me, sitting next to me at the tables where we did our geology work, "Want some water?" Why was she offering me water from the bottle she was drinking from? I hadn't said I was thirsty. I was sure there was LSD in the water. "Sure," I said, and I sipped at it. I took small sips on and off, waiting for it to hit me. I was perfectly happy to trip. After class, I walked around campus, waiting for it to hit me. Finally, I grew bored with this and went home. Was my medication interfering with it? On the bus on the way home, I thought I felt something from it. I thought to myself, "In an hour, I'll know for certain." But an hour later I was home, and I wasn't tripping. I finally realized I had been wrong about the water. But that didn't mean she wouldn't try to drug me in the future; she may have just been getting me comfortable with drinking from her bottle, making sure I wasn't averse to it, and one day—boom—she would hit me with real LSD. I started to grow very afraid of her; at the same time I liked the thought of tripping again.

It had been four years since I had done any drugs, or so much as drunken a beer. Now it has been over 11 years since I have taken LSD, and the hardest thing I have done over those 11 years is smoke pot only twice. I do not like the thought of doing either presently. I do, however, like the thought of beer, whiskey, tequila, rum. It has been only 2 months since I have done that, and I'll probably go back to it soon enough. But that's another story.

63

My first night at Cleo Wallace made me decide right away that the place wasn't for me. I had been at my father's house for perhaps three weeks or a month, since being discharged from Bethesda. I hadn't always been taking the bus across town for day treatment, as I was supposed to, and I had begun to hang out with my old friends and do drugs again. I remember sitting down with my parents and therapist and discussing the options. It was clear I would need long-term treatment; the only question was where. Colorado didn't have that many options, some of which were in the mountains, the closest of which was Cleo Wallace, in Westminster (in between Denver and Boulder). Soon, I found myself being admitted to the residential unit of Cleo Wallace.

Cleo Wallace was a set of one-story buildings widely spread out and set on the edges of town. There was where I was, Unit E, Boys; there were units for girls, units for younger children, the lockdown unit for teens, which I would soon hear about, different school buildings for different units, administrative buildings, etc. There were busy streets and shopping centers if one walked a short distance, and directly next to the well-trimmed grass of the Cleo Wallace grounds was an area of overgrown fields with a brook running through it, a place for bird flocks, foxes, mice, and other wild creatures. To the west one had a clear view of the purple Rocky Mountains, and these seemed clearer and larger from that close point, than they had from southeast Aurora where I grew up, which is an eastern suburb of Denver.

My first night there. I was not told the rules by any staff member, but this duty was delegated to a patient who had particularly proved himself to be good and admired by the staff. He told me about the suits: orange suits were for runaway risks, blue suits were for sexual perpetrators (child molesters) who were thought to be particularly dangerous. He told me about sit-outs: If I did anything wrong, something slight or grave, I would first be told: "Take a seat," by the staff. Then, I would have to sit on the floor facing the wall for five minutes. If I refused, or said a word upon being told to take a seat, or said anything or moved from my spot facing the wall, I would be told, "Go to the quiet room." (The quiet room was a bare room with a door locked from the outside, its floor cold and hard.) If I sat in the corner of the quiet room, and did not move, for ten minutes, I was then let out, and I would have to do my sit-out over again, five minutes facing the wall on the floor, after which I was done. This whole process could be instigated by simply saying, "Shit," in casual conversation. He told me about RAP: restricted activities program. For any given offense, I could be given a set number of RAP hours. I would not be allowed to say a word to anyone. I would have to eat alone. I could not participate in any activities. I would, basically, have to sit at a table for those hours doing nothing but sitting. RAP could last anywhere from two hours to three days; and if I got sat-out in RAP for saying something or moving from my table, I would be given more RAP. He told me about the levels: the more desirable behavior I display, the higher I will move on up in the levels. I will get more and more privileges, more and more freedom, until finally I am discharged. But if I got into trouble, I would be back at the lowest level, and would have to start all over again.

This was all in order to get me to display desirable behavior. This is behavioral mental health, the psychological philosophy that all mental illness is, is undesirable behavior. Correct the behavior, and you've got the illness under control. Thus, behavioral hospitals put their patients in a totalitarian environment where they can punish undesirable behavior with utmost strictness, and reward desirable behavior. Once the patient has displayed considerable desirable behavior, he or she is ready for society, and discharged. There is no need for therapy, or dealing with emotional jungles. Just correct the behavior.

This might have been good for the delinquents and child molesters who were my roommates and companions there, but it was wholly unsuited to my own needs. After all, learning not to say curse words in conversation, learning to obey the staff, learning to be submissive to authority, would avail me nothing when I am out with my friends alone, and they offer me a bong. Even if I succeeded at Cleo Wallace, I would have learned to do everything because I fear punishment, and not because of an inner resolution to improve my life.

But I didn't know this was behaviorist psychological philosophy back then. All I knew was that this place was hard. I hadn't done anything. I hadn't been arrested. Why was I imprisoned? I wasn't willing to accept it. I wouldn't stay, that was for certain. I had gotten kicked out of the rehab once; I would simply refuse to be controlled, refuse to be imprisoned, and they would have to let me go.

But for now, I would simply use a quieter approach. The next night, I asked if I could take a shower. I turned on the water, then slipped out of the bathroom door and into the bedroom nearby. I gathered together two blankets into a pillowcase, and my winter coat; I slipped on all my clothes (three pairs of jeans and several shirts); then I opened the single-story window, and went off into the world. Within five minutes I was off Cleo Wallace grounds. I would later laugh with the staff about the unusual length of that shower, which they only noticed perhaps an hour later.

64

Now I was free, but it was cold (the month of March), and I needed to sleep somewhere. I found an alley behind a supermarket, and situated myself right against the back of the building, under an overhang, where no snow would fall on me as long as it didn't snow hard (it was just starting to sprinkle). The floor was concrete, so I put one blanket under me, and the other over me. Soon, however, I realized how cold the concrete was, how much heat it was sucking out of my body. It was like sleeping on ice. I put both blankets on the ground, and pulled my coat tighter over me to sleep the night. For some reason, I had brought my shower towel with me. Perhaps it was because I remembered reading in *The Hitchhiker's Guide to the Galaxy* about the various uses of towels to the homeless hitchhiker. I do not think towels are particularly useful to the homeless; that was probably the writer's imagination running on and on. But the towel did serve usefully after all. The hood of my coat was merely for the wind, a thin sheet of nylon with tie-strings. I stuffed the towel into it for insulation, then tied it tight around my head. The coat itself was made of some sort of denim, with all sorts of pockets all about it, kind of military style, black. It didn't have any insulation, but it looked good on me, and I was very fond of it. It wasn't, however, good for surviving a night in the cold. A down jacket would have been much better. But I had three pairs of jeans on, and five or six shirts, both short sleeve and long sleeve. I was warm enough, and soon, I fell asleep.

I awoke to the sound of some truck drivers, in the early morning, unloading a truck of goods into the grocery store. I stuffed the blankets and towel into the pillowcase, and walked by them on my way out of the alley. Years later, in a public speech class at Santa Monica College, I would use this experience in one of my speeches. The point of that speech would be to get people to feel sympathy for, and do all they can to help, the homeless. I did not give them the circumstances of why I had slept in the alley; I would only say, "One night I didn't have anywhere to go, and slept in an alley," so maybe the homeless weren't so much different from you and me, etc.

I had a few dollars on me from when I was admitted, which I either had been allowed to keep or had neglected to tell them I had, so I ate breakfast in a fast food burger restaurant. Then I thought, "What can I do?" I knew if I got back to Aurora my friends might be able to help me, but that was about 50 miles away. I know what I should have done: I should have taken the bus. But for some reason, I wasn't thinking straight; I only had three or four dollars left, and I didn't want to waste it on the bus. I didn't either have any idea what bus I should take or how to transfer back to Aurora, but I could have easily asked the bus driver.

Instead of taking the bus, I decided to walk. I knew which direction Aurora was in. It lay off to the southeast, with downtown Denver and hundreds of different neighborhoods in between. I would sleep in alleys as I had the night before, and keep walking, until I got there. This seemed like a sensible plan. I remember being kind of dazed and just going to the next thing: walk down this street, walk these next blocks, without any idea that I may have to sleep in Denver's worst neighborhoods if I went the wrong route. The neighborhood I was in didn't scare me, and I wasn't really thinking of the future.

Around noon, a van pulled up beside me, with a single woman in it. She opened the door. "Get in!" she said. "I'm from Cleo Wallace." It was very attractive to just get in. Then, I could leave all these homeless worries behind me. I knew that before I got to Aurora, I would be hungry; and just as sure as I would be hungry, I would be cold. I got in the front seat of the van, and she drove me back to Cleo Wallace. Apparently, they had been driving all around looking for me. Well, they had found me. Now, it was time to face my punishment.

65

When my sister told me, about five years ago, that her childhood friend Chelsea (or Chessie, as we called her) interned at Cleo Wallace after I had gone, when she was in college, at first I thought, "How could she do such a thing!" I still had only anger for the staff at Cleo Wallace.

This childhood friend of my sister's was always around the house, and she was often my playmate as well as my sister's, from the time we were little children. After some reflection, I thought, when considering her internship at Cleo Wallace, "That poor girl!" The Chessie I remembered would not be prepared for what she would meet in the patients at Cleo Wallace.

The staff, after all, were expected to take down patients who refused to go to the quiet room when directed, and this was, at least in the lockdown unit, almost a daily occurrence. Someone or other was always being taken down, and some of the patients did more than wrestle; sometimes it would happen that they would land hard swings in the faces of male and female mental health workers alike. Such a totalitarian environment, in which one has to become so submissive and repressed in order to go up in the levels, often leads to moments of the opposite reaction: I am going to do what I want, and to hell with the consequences. I have now only sympathy for the mental health workers at Cleo Wallace; most of them were only trying to make a living with the best job they could get, and though some were working on college degrees, most did not already have one.

I'm not sure how it happened when I got managed for the first time there. But I was determined now to go on a campaign of non-cooperation such as I had seen in that popular movie on Gandhi's life that won so many Academy Awards. That movie had made refusing to follow direction, and forcing the oppressor into violence against you, seem to make the oppressor the unjustified one and you the noble one, seem to be a means to conquer any oppression. I thought it had to work. The staff would be forced to take me down, they would become more unjustified and villainous the more violent I forced them to get with me, and I would finally be justified and conquer. This was how all powerless people ought to deal with oppressors, I believed; it had seemed so easy in the movie, as long as one is willing to go through the pain, and everything had seemed so simple and black-and-white with my version of Gandhi's philosophy.

Once I was in my orange suit, sitting at that table serving my two days or so of RAP, having been demoted to the lowest level, I forced a takedown by simply refusing to go to the quiet room when directed (I had probably been sat-out and said something). Takedowns in this institution were a little different than in Bethesda. Here, the point wasn't so much as to get you incapacitated so you could be taken by gurney to seclusion. It was more to make you suffer and become willing to walk to the quiet room. They did not carry you there, but let you up after the takedown, and told you to walk to the quiet room.

Their method of takedown was to lift you up, bring your arms behind your back, and slam you onto your chest on the floor. Then one of the men would lie across your back, crushing your lungs so that it was hard to breathe, with your hands painfully twisted behind you, for about five minutes, until you were let up and told to walk to the quiet room.

I remember one time in the lockdown unit, when the staff finally gave a response after having been repeatedly told by the patients that they couldn't breathe during a takedown. A female mental health worker responded to the whole community during a community meeting. She was a very bitter woman in her forties, small but strong and harsh, who had no patience with any kind of misbehavior. Her hair was dark, short, and curly, her teeth were terribly malformed as if she had never received the braces she desperately needed, and she was very ugly, thick, and stocky. "If you can say you can't breathe," she told us, "that means you can breathe. So we know when you say, 'I can't breathe,' during a physical management, that you are breathing, and everything is all right." This was the woman who was socked in the face by a small, angry, and fierce patient during a takedown once, after which the entire community was informed that assault charges had been filed with the police. Upon hearing this, I thought, "It's legal for them to attack us, but illegal for us to make any physical defense?" But now, I think it was a good thing not to tolerate that. The staff, after all, were only usually unskilled working men and women, just showing up to work every day; and no one wants to go to a job where she will get socked in the teeth. That's a bad day at work.

Anyway, back at Unit E, residential, I was taken down. After he told me, "I am going to let you up, and you are going to walk into the quiet room," I didn't respond. He let me up. I stood, and walked out the side door, and began walking away slowly from the residential unit. He followed behind me, speaking, with a strain of panic in his voice. I hadn't struggled when he took me down the first time, and had just taken it; he didn't want to hurt me again, but I was leaving him no choice. Two of them followed behind me, and I heard the one named Stuart, saying to me, "If you don't turn around now, we're going to have to manage you again." I didn't turn around or say a word, but kept my slow pace, walking away. Soon, I was lifted up, my arms were brought behind my back, and I was slammed down into the grass. They held me down for a little while, until two or three of them decided to carry me to the quiet room.

66

My mother belongs to a book group of somewhere around 12 women, who all read a common book every month, and meet to discuss it. Such a thing is very common nowadays, especially for women of my mother's class and age. Of the 12 or so women who belong to this book group (my mother tells me), one has an adopted son who is schizophrenic and lives with her, and another has two daughters, both of whom are married and have bipolar disorder.

My mother, having me for a son, is able to discuss my schizophrenia and its effect on her (if she ever does; I don't ask her) with these other women, without any shame. I suspect she does; she is always telling me news of the other women's mentally ill children, so the other women do anyway.

Schizophrenia is so common, chances are that the reader has known someone with a child, relative, or close friend who was schizophrenic; chances are even greater that the reader has been in contact with a schizophrenic for some reason, at work or in college, without ever knowing it. Why, then, do so many people not even have any idea what schizophrenia is, why do so many people think it has to do with multiple personalities, why do so many people think "psychosis" means some sort of animal, murdering mentality? I believe the answer is that these associates of the reader (if I may make assumptions) who have schizophrenic relatives keep it secret; the schizophrenics the reader has met, in some sort of business, dating, or scholarly relationship, have kept quiet about their illness. No one knows what schizophrenia is, because no one will admit to having it; no one will admit to having it, because no one knows what it is, but whatever it is (they think), it is an incredibly shameful and fearsome thing. I do not know what to do about this; but I am not going to be the first, on, say, my university campus, to start telling strangers I have schizophrenia. That would only make me a miserable outcast.

I will, however, write this book. I will not use a pseudonym. Like me or not, I'm here to tell you: I am not ashamed. I am tired of being ashamed of being sick. I am not ashamed.

67

I was 17 when I was admitted to Cleo Wallace and I would be well over 18 when I was discharged. Not only was I at my sexual peak, but I had been sexually repressed all my life, and I was forced to repress further in that environment. No more *Penthouse* or *Playboy* magazines, no more satisfying masturbation sessions with relaxed fantasies and some sort of comfortable lubricant. The best I could manage was what everyone did: a quick busted nut in the shower, and the secondary sting of the soap later on the tip of the urethra. I know that all the young men in Unit E did the same as I, and I found it somewhat amusing that none of them would admit to it. "Come on," I would say, "you spank the monkey in the shower just like me." "Oh no," they would say, "spanking the monkey is sick." "What do you think?" I would say. "Do the others do it?" "Yeah," they would say, "all the others do it; but not me; I would never do such a thing." One day one of them asked me, "How often do you jack off?" "About twice a week," I said. I was very overmedicated. "The people in my hall do it every day," he said; "I hear them, and they take such long showers." "Do you do so too?" I said. "Oh no, I never do."

I am thinking of the chances I had at Cleo Wallace to actually express my desires. There was one fine-looking young man at Unit E named Christopher; we became good friends. He introduced me to the band Ministry, which I very much liked, and he sometimes spent time doing up my long blond hair however his creativity inspired him. He seemed to take a special interest in me, and I appreciated him very much. One day he put his arm around me as we were watching TV together on a couch. I put my arm around him, and we began to cuddle. Suddenly one of the other boys looked around his shoulder at us and said, "What's going on here? They must be fairies." We stopped at once and laughed it off.

But within a few days, one day when we came back from the school Christopher was gone. He had left a note on my pillow explaining that he had been sent to another institution. So much for that.

There was another friend I had there who was a skinhead (or former skinhead), who had close-cropped hair and bad skin, and whose looks I was very much reminded of by the photographs and newsreels of Timothy McVeigh. He admitted to me that he was bisexual, and made it known that he was attracted to me; but I was never attracted to him, so I always made a joke out of it, and didn't make myself available to him. It just wasn't there.

Maybe 7 months later, at the lockdown unit where the boys and girls are in the same hospital, I had a chance to actually get involved with girls. There was one girl who was new there, probably just 15 or 16 years old. As soon as we got to know each other, she began passing me very obscene, pornographic notes that read things like, "I want to take your cock into my mouth," and other very detailed proposals. Soon enough, I sneaked out of my room one night as my roommate was sleeping, across the well-lit dayroom with the nurses' station window looking down on it, and into her room. She was shocked that I had actually shown up. At first, she kissed me. It was a disgusting kiss; it had the exaggerated movements of someone who wants to pretend she is passionate, but really has no feeling at all. It was a prostitute's kiss, utterly false. Suddenly she said, "Hide under the bed!" I did so. The staff went through and checked our rooms several times in the night, but just now no one came. Then she told me plainly: I think you'd better go, I don't want to get into trouble. I had already suspected as much, so I went back into my room.

This time, as I crossed the dayroom, I was seen. A mental health worker came to my door and said, "What are you doing out of your room?" "I'm looking for my guitar," I said. "You know you can't have that now," he said, and then left me.

The last time was with a 16-year-old, good-looking blond girl with very nice breasts. We would often eat and talk together, and she seemed to like me well enough. We sometimes played a game where we would stare at each other, and then try to guess what the expressions we had seen in each other's eyes were trying to say. I always grew disturbed staring straight into her eyes, as people often do; but we only laughed over it. There was a little place under the metal stairway that led to the yard where we could go during yard time, which was out of the visual range of the staff, and steal kisses together. One night, the night before the day she was to be discharged, I was awoken by her just after dawn. She had sneaked into my room, just as I had sneaked into that other girl's room a few months before.

My roommate was an 18- or 19-year-old autistic man at the time, from whose mouth came the same nonsensical phrases over and over again. "Sushi," he would repeat, "suuushi." Of all the patients at Cleo Wallace, I pitied the autistic patients the most. Many of the patients were there on court order, as an alternative to juvenile hall, and some, I suspect, arrived there as a condition of some sort of parole (especially the sexual perpetrators). The two autistic patients I knew there were completely helpless and innocent; they did not deserve to be in the same place as criminals, with the same rules as are needed to control criminal behavior. Neither, for that matter, did I.

As my roommate slept away in his bed, this girl and I kissed, and she took off all her clothes. I was already only in my underwear. I caressed her breasts and said to her, "Let's have oral sex." "No," she said, "I don't want to. Let's make love, though." "But what if you get pregnant?" I said. "I'll just have an abortion," she said.

Well, that was that: it was time to go to work. But I didn't want to go to work. All this was eating at me—the autistic man sleeping a few feet from us, the suddenness of her coming, the word "abortion" and the images it brought to mind, the fact that any second now a mental health worker would be walking in on us. I did not feel aroused, and, looking down, she and I could both see that I wasn't aroused. "What's wrong?" she said. I tried to play it off. "Nothing," I said, and I tried kissing her again. I was very much relieved when, seconds later, I heard a female mental health worker's voice behind me, *"Jesus! Take a seat!"*

68

In my freshman year in high school, one day a sophomore came up to me and said, "You see that girl across the hall?" He pointed to a girl with fluffy blond hair, a Roman nose, and very pale skin, who always dressed in hip Goth fashion. "I'm a friend of hers. She likes you." This girl's friends kept trying to set me up with her after that; apparently she had some sort of crush on me that just wouldn't go away. Girls had had crushes on me before; but I had always been too ashamed of my own desire, and frightened of making a fool of myself, to act on them; and these crushes had gone out of the girls' minds as quickly as they had come. But this girl was persistent. All that year and the next, I found myself at parties with her, smoking pot with her friends in the school parking lot, out drinking with her, and doing different things with her. Never once did I act on this crush of hers; she was one year ahead of me, and her friends and she were alien to me; I was very frightened of the whole thing. My friends made me ashamed of being with her, and made immature jokes that those girls' Gothic, stylish, very baggy pants made it look like, well, they were very immature jokes. It would have, actually, been good for me to have gotten involved with her. But though, on several occasions, such as when I was drinking beer with her late at night in a park, every indication was that she wanted me to kiss her, I was always too terrified to make the first move.

One night, we were at a keg party with at least a hundred people, most of them strangers, in some strange house. I'm not quite sure how we ended up there together, but none of my normal group of friends was there. In a small room down some stairs, I found myself passing around a pipe with her and about three other people, including the hip black guy who had told me in the beginning, "See that girl? She likes you." As soon as I was stoned and completely self-conscious, suddenly the others left, and it was just I and this girl, alone. My instinct was to move with the crowd—everyone was moving to another room, ought not we to move too? Then I realized I was meant to make my move, and I was terrified. My throat and lips were dry as bone from the pot, my gut was stirring inside of me; and there she was, her lips parted, silent, overwhelming me. I just wanted to flee, and so that's what I did. I suddenly burst from the room up the stairs, to pass a drunk stranger on his way down, who said, "Hey? What's going on down here?" I didn't answer him, but went on by and into a situation safer and more comfortable.

Had she kissed me, I would have gone ahead with it; but as for making the first move, I kept telling myself, "Don't put too much weight on reality; it could suddenly turn around and be the complete opposite of what you think it is." She was shy and I was shy; it was a sad state of affairs; we seemed perfect for each other, after all.

When I entered my junior year psychotic, she and her friends I'm sure could tell. My friend Pat, who knew her, kept saying to me, "Jennele" (that was her name) "really wants to talk to you, give her a call." He even handed me her number, but I never called. What could she do for me, anyway? I was beyond needing a girlfriend.

But somehow, after I was in Cleo Wallace, she got in contact with me. I used to talk to her on the phone at Unit E, and she even put up with my apathetic way of answering every question with one word and never filling an awkward silence myself. I told her I was schizophrenic. She told me she wanted to study psychology when she went to college. I wondered if I had had anything to do with that decision.

Anyway, we did finally kiss, though a relationship at this point was impossible, and I have to admit I wouldn't have had much to offer had we started one. I went on a date with her when I was on pass one weekend. She, one of her female friends whom I already knew, and my brother went along. My brother told me, "No drinking," and was there to make sure I didn't get into any trouble, so we finally turned around and dropped him off back at my mother's house. I knew I was going to get into trouble, but I could deal with it, and I wanted one really good night. Jennele, her friend (who I must admit I was always more attracted to than I was to Jennele) and I went out driving around and drinking beers. I don't really remember all the places we went. All I know was that Jennele was willing to put up with my schizophrenic personality, and found something of value in it.

Before we had dropped my brother off, we had gone to a fast food restaurant for dinner. I had been staring down at my food and not saying much. Suddenly I said something and realized a great chunk of sandwich had come out of my mouth and fallen onto the table as I said it. My medication caused drooling, and I was struggling not to drool. I don't remember if she noticed me drool or not.

But none of that seemed to matter when we got home late, and they were dropping me at my mother's to be taken back to Cleo Wallace for my punishment. Jennele put her arms around me as we stood by the car, and said, "I don't want you to have to go back to that awful place." I leaned forward and began to kiss her, and we kissed a good while. My mother was inside giving me my time with her before she came out to scold me. Scold me as she did later on, I was very happy. I knew that this was not the beginning of a relationship, that I would probably never kiss Jennele again; but I had overcome a great terror of mine, and found it was only a soft, lovely, and loving creature.

69

About a year ago, last winter, I put on my fireman's coat my father had given me from when he was helping his in-law manage a fire gear factory, and walked about a quarter-mile to the Kentucky Inn. There's a bar closer to me with similarly cheap prices—the Candlelight Tavern—but I always see bikers going in there, so I was a little afraid of that one. I rarely go to bars.

I had decided on only one beer at the bar before I had left. I had decided, Yes, I'm drinking too much lately, I will drink one beer and leave. Well, I sat down and ordered my single Budweiser. The bartender said it was something like $2.25. "I was in here before," I said, "and it was only $1.50." "That's draft beer," said the bartender, who took my bottle away, which he had already opened, then set a cup of draft beer before me.

A woman sat down two stools from me. She was only slightly over-weight—so slight it only gave her hips more form, her body more…more *body*. She was obviously one of those white trash girls who goes out to get drunk on weekends, goes out to get laid. I do not mind white trash, if white trash is only defined as whites who are below middle class. You saw them in this bar all the time—the men bearded, chain smoking, sometimes even nervous, the women saying things to their female friends like, "Look who's got a new drinking buddy—you do!" and slamming down beers, with no taste for wine. I do not mind such people. But they have one thing I don't like…they are *people*. I do not like people, any people.

This woman obviously wanted me to say something to her. My mind was a complete blank. My beer was making me dizzy, and my dizziness made me self-conscious. Certainly all my social ineptitude of my past was coming back to me, how all my life I have never even had a steady relationship, how I didn't have any idea about how to go about having a relationship. I knew that even should end up taking this woman home with me, I would not have the capacity to see it as lightly as she, that it would disturb me with unpleasant emotions the next day as much as give me pleasure the night before.

The bartender said, "It's real quiet around here." I hated him for saying this. Now the pressure was on me.

I finished my beer, and walked out the door. I was happy to stop at just one beer.

70

But back to why I was in Cleo Wallace for so long.

After I was carried to the quiet room, I was willing to stay in there forever. The floor of this quiet room was wood, and so I curled up on the floor, shut my eyes, and began to wait it out. After perhaps an hour the staff did not know what to do. The quiet room was in the back of the office, and Unit E had only one—they could not afford to have it occupied all day, as they may need it. I could hear Bill—who was in charge—on the phone with somebody. "He's just lying there in the fetal position…" Bill was a kindhearted man in his 30s with a false left leg below the knee. He'd had his real leg removed during cancer treatments years earlier. He was easy enough to get along with, but if he had to manage you, he could pin you down all on his own in a flash, as I learned before I left there.

I took this comment about the fetal position as an insult. I was merely trying to make myself comfortable on the hard floor, was this any reason to call me an infant? In any case, they didn't know what to do with me. When Mike's shift came up, he thought he could handle this situation with ease—or not ease, precisely, but roughness.

The door was opened, and I was told to go down the short set of stairs to the common room, and do my sit-out. I walked down there, sat facing the wall, then lay back, so that my entire back and head were resting on the floor. "Sit up," said Mike, standing right behind me, "or you will be helped!" I did not sit up. He took a hold of my long hair with both hands, and yanked me into a sitting position. As soon as he let go, I went back down. He yanked me up again. This happened three times, until he decided to pick me up, and slam me down on my chest as the others had done, to manage me. Then I was shown back into the quiet room, where I settled myself again on the floor. As I was walking there, I said to Mike, "You pulled my hair." "Tell someone who cares," he said.

I didn't know it then, but Mike would end up being one of my closest friends at Cleo Wallace. He was a tall, burly man who taught martial arts and was working on his undergraduate degree in psychology. He was of Irish descent and had red hair that he kept tied into a neat ponytail at the back of his head, and a bushy red beard. His cruelty only came from the behavioral philosophy he so adhered to—to be merciful to disobedient patients was only to do them disservice. The crueler you were, the less you tolerated undesirable behavior, the healthier the patient would be when released. His cruelty, in his eyes, was the deepest kindness.

But I didn't know this then. I did not fear him—I despised him. I did not fear what anyone might to do me there—the worse they treated me, the more unjustified they became, and the more justified I became. And I had, after all, been shown back to the quiet room. I had made Mike fail—that was good enough for me.

That very day, I was transferred to the lockdown unit. I walked there compliantly, escorted by Mike and Bill. According to behavioral philosophy, my disobedience was the sign of the deepest, most chronic psychotic mental illness. The strange thing was, though, that I didn't feel psychotic at all.

71

I was just reading the *New York Times* Book Review on the web. There was a review of a recent book, *Gracefully Insane* by Alex Beam, about a famous mental institution for the well to do. Holly Brubach wrote the review (*New York Times,* February 24, 2002), and titled the review: "'Gracefully Insane': The Thoroughbred Crazies." If the *New York Times* doesn't see anything wrong with excluding us as "crazies", should we really expect basic respect from people we meet, if we tell them we have schizophrenia? Should we think that the day we can tell a first date the most overpowering fact about us—we have schizophrenia—without making her run, is coming anytime soon?

72

At the lockdown hospital unit, I had the maximum of two or three days of RAP to serve. I at first decided to wait it out in the quiet room again (they had two quiet rooms there), until I found that they were perfectly happy to let me stay in there forever, letting me out periodically to use the bathroom, and I would never be allowed to see the therapist I'd had at Bethesda, whom I had always found so sympathetic to me. I finally sat in the corner of the quiet room for the required time, then did my sit-out facing the wall. What was next wasn't much better. I was on RAP, so I wasn't allowed to speak to anyone, and I had to sit on a chair facing the wall, not allowed to read or do anything, until my RAP had been served. I ate my meals on a little tray they put before me in my place facing the wall, and wasn't allowed to participate in any activities, such as exercise, yard time, room time, or anything else. I was not given a room, but would have to sleep on a mattress on the floor of the dayroom, with the lights only dimmed a little, and the night staff talking and walking around like they always did. If I said anything to the staff or anyone else without raising my hand and being called upon, I would be sat out, and get one more hour of RAP.

When my therapist heard of all that had happened, and came to see me, she seemed horrified at what had happened to me. I showed her the rug scrapes on my elbows, which looked like I had skinned them on concrete. That was when I told her I was going on a hunger strike. "Do you want to end up on an IV?" she said. She was the only one I told about the hunger strike. I suspect that's why the rest of the staff only ignored it when I wouldn't eat. "When he gets hungry enough, he'll eat," they probably said. They were right.

My meeting with my therapist was short. I wouldn't see her again for about a year, when my new therapist would finally let her see me. I was never told that the therapist I had so trusted, Helen, was no longer allowed to see me. One day, I saw her through the Plexiglas window of the nurses' station. I immediately went up and waited to be called to see her. I never was, and I had only seen her there for a brief moment. When I was allowed to meet with her a year later, after it was already decided that I was going to a hospital in California, she said to me, "I came to see you. But they would not let me speak to you." I suspect she protested too much the rough treatment I had received, but I'll never know for sure.

After my hunger strike was over, after my RAP was over, I was allowed into my room. My roommate at the time was a tough, but not violent, stocky Chilean American. I was later in Unit E with him, and he, like me, could take a lot of physical pain, and would refuse to follow direction if he was angry enough even when it meant being physically managed on stairs. One night, when he was sleeping, I took one of the heavy metal chairs we used to sit at our desks to write letters or read, and threw it as hard as I could at the Plexiglas window. I was trying to run away again, and it was a one-story building. The chair bounced off the window without cracking it, making a very loud banging noise. The Chilean opened his eyes and glanced at me, then closed them again and went back to sleep. I threw the chair vainly one or two more times, even harder, and then decided to go back to bed before I got into trouble.

Next came my "suicide" attempts. I was not suicidal; I did not want to die. I was not even trying to die. To tell the truth, I don't know what I was doing. I think I was angry at everything, and unable to hurt anyone but myself. I was still working under the Gandhi Theory, and so somehow I supposed if I hurt myself, they would be hurting me, the unjust ones.

I took a plastic knife such as we were given with every meal. These plastic knives weren't very sharp, but had teeth. Plastic is harder than skin, so it will cut into skin when sawed back and forth over it a few dozen times. I sawed at my wrist during room time. I sawed for a whole hour. There was blood, I cut down to the veins, but the blue veins sat there naked, not covered by any skin, buried in the tendons my knife wouldn't cut. I was never able to slice one of those arteries with the plastic knife. Once I got down to the tendons, each sawing motion made a loud *zip* noise as the teeth of the knife rubbed against the toughness of my tendons. The Chilean lay there in bed trying to ignore this loud *zip, zip, zip* as I sat by the window a few feet from him sawing at my wrist. When I was done, I had two large openings in my wrist, through which one could see naked tendons and veins; the knife was bloody, my wrist was bloody, but it wasn't flowing blood; just blood from the capillaries in the skin. I showed it to the Chilean and he said, "That's gross". He never said anything more about it. I'm sure I was disturbing him, but he seemed willing to ignore it. I can still see the thin white scars on my right hand wrist now.

73

The question that is on my mind about my time at Cleo Wallace, which was characterized by only a brief period of obedience, and the rest of the time complete disobedience punctuated by escapes and attempted escapes, is whether my disobedience was truly a psychotic symptom, as the staff supposed. I believe, though it wasn't as clearly psychotic as my telepathic delusion, that it may have been, especially in the beginning. I had this self-righteous mentality, coming from everything I had been taught in grade school about truth, justice, and the American way, that I was being locked up and oppressed, that I had neither committed a crime nor been put on trial, and yet here I was imprisoned. I felt it was my duty to fight this injustice with non-cooperation, just as Martin Luther King had fought injustice in the same way. I had an inflated sense of my own righteousness in the face of my oppressors (I never, after all, perpetrated violence against them, though they were violent with me all the time). In reality I could have been discharged three months after I had arrived had I merely, from the beginning, followed all the rules and worked the system. As it was, I was there for over a year.

But their entire psychological philosophy failed me. You cannot beat a delusion out of a schizophrenic. You cannot punish psychosis away. The more they were violent with me, or subjected me to psychological punishment, the more I became, in my mind, the righteous victim standing up to injustice. According to their philosophy, I ought to have ended up disliking the punishment so much that I would leave all psychotic behavior behind. But in fact their punishment only served to justify my psychotic beliefs, and so I went on disobeying them. This would have simply gone on forever, had I not been transferred to a hospital that was not a behavioral institution better suited for treating juvenile criminality and delinquency. By the time I was discharged, my therapist (Jamie) was telling my parents I would probably have to remain institutionalized the rest of my life. Nine months after I was transferred to a hospital more suited to my needs, I was renting my own place and attending Santa Monica College; and though I've had brief hospital stays, I've never looked back since.

When the police took me to the county hospital in 1999 (it's a long story I'll probably get into later), the hospital staff was angry at them for bringing me, as I obviously didn't need to be there at all, and all their beds were full. They let me go the next morning.

74

I wrote an emailed letter to the *New York Times* Book Review editors about that title of their review: "'Gracefully Insane': The Thoroughbred Crazies". The letter wasn't psychotic or angry; it was clear, controlled, and focused. But after I had written the letter I reread it and thought. I realized that with my two chapters that discuss stigma and past oppression of schizophrenics in my last book (unpublished), and the sections that discuss it in this manuscript, I am developing the same righteous-oppressed-man-standing-up-for-justice mentality I had in that hospital. I will be a crusader against stigma, the voice of the oppressed mentally ill, the one to finally point out that we, as a minority, have been subject throughout history to as much cruelty as any other oppressed minority. All this is true enough, but what about this "mission" I am developing to go up against it?

It seems to me that I'm starting to inflate my own importance in history and society, just as I used to with my former religious saint complex, just as I did in that hospital when I viewed myself as unjustly held captive, righteously going up against my oppressors.

It is a cruel catch-22 the schizophrenic is in. On the one hand, his oppression as a minority is real (abuse in hospitals is real; frontal lobotomies and seclusion are truly oppression; schizophrenics are still discriminated against when it comes to getting employment). He lives in a culture that excludes him as one of the "crazies" and "psychos" as the television is always telling him. On the other hand, if he actually complains to society, raises up his voice, tries to stand up against it, he will do so in not such a sane way; there will be a persecution complex; there will be his inflated sense of importance. Even with medications, which now allow the schizophrenic at least the ability to speak for himself rationally, he is not completely sane; there can never be a Martin Luther King of mental illness. This is the problem, and the solution is as it has always been. It is up to the normies sympathetic to the mentally ill to change society; the schizophrenic still isn't healthy enough for that. We will be subject to cruelty no more not when we are able to speak for ourselves, but when society decides not to be so cruel toward us. The issue is in your hands, not mine; I'm just a sick man trying to get by, unable to brush his teeth and shower every day, afraid of speaking to people in a bar.

I hope the *New York Times* doesn't publish my letter. I don't think I have much to worry about, though.

75

Don't romanticize my life. Don't make me into the heroic victim. Don't let me make you wish, at some hidden place in your heart, that you could say you have been once in an institution. Schizophrenia is not romantic. Abuse in mental hospitals does not make me a heroic victim. There is nothing good in it: if you have never been locked up in a mental hospital, I would say: good for you, that's one good point for you and none for me. There is nothing romantic about psychosis: it is painful, it is anguishing, it is ugly. I wouldn't wish it on anybody, and I am no more heroic for going through it, than is a man who crosses a street, unfortunately gets hit by a car by pure chance, and becomes paralyzed for the rest of his life. We ought not to say of such a life, "He's such a strong and noble man," but rather, "That's so unfortunate, what happened to him—I hope it doesn't happen to me."

Don't expect noble sentences at the end of this memoir about how determined I am to get everything out of life notwithstanding my mental illness, about how I am determined to beat it and never lose hope, about how I will overcome all odds and any discouragement. I think I've made it clear what a coward I am. I am afraid of any type of social interaction, afraid of the social interaction needed to do something as simple as bus tables in a restaurant. I am perfectly happy to give up any hope of marriage, family, career, and graduate education. If I could just write the rest of my life, stay locked inside my apartment, watch my step-niece grow up from afar, grow old and lonely, die in this very apartment never having ventured into the world, I would be happy to do so. I have realized that I won't get everything out of life, and it is only the stubborn and self-exalted one who will refuse to die of cancer when told by everyone he is dying of cancer, and then die of cancer. I would say it would be braver to accept death, face it, and submit to it. I submit to my schizophrenia. It has broken me down, so that at a dinner with strangers I suddenly find myself terrified that they hear my thoughts; so that if I converse with an Egyptian on a bus I'm thinking to myself, "He's an Al Qaeda fugitive who thinks I'm undercover FBI". I'm the one you see on the street, his hair a mess, his clothes dirty, waiting for a bus; this one would only be very naïve to expect everything out of life. It would be more courageous of him to accept what he may not exactly like: he will have to live a life that most people would not find happiness in, and find his own scaled-back, humbler, and simpler happiness in it. And yes, I consider myself, in general, happy. I haven't overcome; I have become satisfied with less.

76

As the best therapist I ever had, who knew me the best, remarked once to me when I was in California, I have neither the background nor the personality of the typical self-mutilator. Self-mutilation, which I do not really understand myself, usually has something to do with child abuse in one's past, and is a kind of addiction or compulsion. Some of the girls in the lockdown unit of Cleo Wallace were such compulsive self-mutilators, scratching scabs into their skin or rubbing the skin till it bled with pencil erasers. I somehow thought it was curious how you could make such profound wounds by merely scratching the skin back and forth a long time with the fingernail, so I tried it. It didn't hurt, really. I kept it up as a habit at Cleo Wallace; I'm not sure why, I didn't have any compulsion to do it; I suppose I was merely trying to fit in with my peers. I was never punished for it, though the others were; my therapist probably thought it was best to ignore such behavior, thinking if I got no attention for it I would stop. She was right. Had they punished me for it, I would have done more of it as an act of defiance.

After I left Cleo Wallace, I forgot all about self-mutilation, with only a few permanent marks on my flesh to remind me. But after I was discharged, after I had been living in my own apartment several years, one night, shortly after I had gotten back from my trip to Copper Canyon, I was in a deep depression.

When I had gotten home, I had again mixed up my antipsychotic medication with my antidepressant. When I got back I started to take my antipsychotic (of which I had plenty waiting for me at home), and this time, thinking I had already gone so long without my antidepressant at Copper Canyon (when I had really gone without my antipsychotic) I went without my antidepressant. You wonder how I could make such a simple error for so long, how it was that I still didn't look at the labels on the bottles. But I had been in a very confused state ever since the trip to Mexico had begun, and by now I was sleeping for 24 hours at a time, and staying awake for the same; I was very confused. It was only a week after the depression that followed, after the psychosis at Copper Canyon had ended, that I really looked at the labels, and looked carefully at the appearance of the capsules, and realized what had happened.

Anyway, I was in this deep depression that had already lasted several days. I was apathetic toward everything, and did nothing but flip through the channels on the TV for as long as I was awake. At one point, I was sitting out on the balcony. We had a dirty table and a chair out there, and there was a big pile of the cans and bottles we were saving to recycle in the corner. We accumulated cans and bottles for a long time before we got around to taking them to the recycle station, so the pile in the corner got very high. This was just before California stopped paying a good price for recycled cans, and I remember the time I took them in and found, disappointed, that what was normally worth at least $20 was now worth about $4.50.

That week of depression, I would often sit on the guard wall of the second story balcony, my back to the outside, and lift my legs up straight, so that the knees weren't bent and the legs stuck straight out, just daring fate to make me lose my balance. This was less a suicide attempt and more an indifferent curiosity at what would happen.

But right now I was sitting at the table. There was a pack of my roommate's cigarettes and a lighter sitting on the table. I didn't smoke back then, but I lit up a cigarette, only to press the burning tobacco into the inside of my forearm. I held it there several seconds, then took it away. The pain really wasn't that bad. I have no idea why I did it. I think I was just curiously manipulating nature, trying to see, with complete indifference, what would happen if I touched this with that, moved the other here or there. If I got burned, if it hurt, that didn't matter in the least: I didn't care at all. I was just curious, that's all. Is this really that insane?

77

I do not know precisely how many times I ran away from Cleo Wallace. I remember going to sleep in an alley one night—it was dark, it wasn't cold this time, I was afraid. I saw sheets of broken glass sitting in a dumpster, broken glass on the concrete—and suddenly I was terrified, and went back to Cleo Wallace. I remember wandering the streets around Cleo Wallace on another night, and being picked up by a mental health worker who had happened to see me on his way in to work, and driven indifferently back into captivity.

I only escaped once from the lockdown hospital unit, and I remember distinctly that this was a separate occasion. It was after I had been discharged and then readmitted, after I had gone through my one period of obedience and then found that I fell apart as soon as I was released. I was in the lockdown hospital unit, in the orange suit for runaways. My therapist came to see me, and we went on a walk outside as we talked. I didn't have any shoelaces on, so I couldn't run far without leaving my shoes behind. We sat at a picnic table and talked. "I want out," I remember saying. "When can I expect to be discharged?" "That won't happen for a good while," she said. As if that were my cue, I slipped off my shoes, put them in my hand, and ran as fast as I could through the Cleo Wallace grounds, the summer grass soft under my feet. I made it as far as Aurora that time.

Three times I made it back to Aurora. I do not know how many nights I was away. My memory is so confused I only remember actually begging for bus money and taking the bus there once—but I must have all three times, because none of my friends ever drove out to pick me up, and it would have been impossible to walk.

I know I made it to Aurora three times because I remember three separate ways I was brought back. One was when I went to my mother's house, after either sleeping outside in the safe Aurora neighborhoods or spending the night with my friend Frederick. I was there to pick up my bicycle. My mother was angry and demanded I go back to Cleo Wallace, but I only ignored her, and began to pump air into my bicycle tire at my leisure. Of course, the police showed up to my surprise. I asked the officer, "Am I under arrest?" and when he said no I arrogantly turned and began to walk away. He got my arm in such a position that he could inflict immense pain just by lifting, and showed my stepfather how to do it. Then he handed my stepfather my arm, and I was driven back to Cleo Wallace in the back of my stepfather's van (my mother driving), with my stepfather holding my arm in that painful position to my right. It was all very humiliating.

The second time was when I was heading out to Cherry Creek Reservoir with camping gear I had picked up from my father's house, intent on camping out, at least for the time being. My father was coming along with me, just following me, refusing to let me go but unable to stop me. He had called the police as I had left the house, though I didn't know it. As we were walking, he said, "Those are my shoes!" pointing at my shoes. It was true: he had given me his old shoes, just as he always did, since they were my size and he threw them out before they were even worn. I gave him the shoes, and went along in my socks. I was no thief, after all.

To make a long story short, I was picked up by the police at Cherry Creek Reservoir. They ran my driver's license, and found a warrant for my arrest (failure to appear in court on a drunk driving charge, which was later dismissed), and my parents had to bail me out of jail to take me back to Cleo Wallace.

The third time was when I went straight to my mother's house as soon as I made it to Aurora, and let her drive me right back. This was the time I had made it away while on a walk with my therapist, my shoes held in hand. I knew by then it was vain to run away; there was really nowhere I could go. By then my escape attempts were only something to do, something to focus on, and when they actually bore fruit, the success they had was absolutely useless. This is the time I remember clearly bumming the change at a supermarket and taking the bus back to Aurora. I went to a pay phone first and called my friend Ramsey collect, and asked for a ride. "I can't give you a ride," he told me. I think he just didn't want to help me run away from what was probably good for me. I was in an orange suit, but I had put my button-up undershirt over the top portion of it, and the bottom portion had the ankles cut off, like cutoff shorts. I didn't have any laces in my shoes, but I may have fit in well enough, especially when I transferred buses in downtown Denver.

As soon as I rang the bell and walked into my mother's house, she told me how worried she had been, and that she had called my brother, who was on the phone. "You made it back to Aurora?" he said when I picked up the phone, *"And you're in an orange suit?"*

But there was one memory I have in particular. I have just arrived to my friend Frederick's house. I am showing him my wrist scar and telling him of the terrible things I have undergone. His mother is there too: Frederick and I are sitting in his room on the bed, facing a large window. His mother says, "You can't kill yourself anyway by cutting in that direction; the only way is to—but I shouldn't tell you." Then she is very sympathetic to me, telling me how I have been mistreated, how my family and those doctors won't show me the slightest kindness. "How long has it been since you have had a hug?" she says. "Do they even give you hugs there? I'll bet not." I stand and she gives me a hug. I start to get an erection, and she can feel it. She lets me go and says, "Don't." "Don't what?" I say, embarrassed. "Don't," she repeats. Sheepishly, I sit back down, humiliated.

One time, I was allowed to walk right out the door. This was on my 18th birthday, when I realized more than my parents' signature was needed to keep me there. I was at Unit E, and told them: I want to leave, and I'm 18. They discussed among themselves what to do for a few hours, and then Stuart told me: All right, go. I left, penniless, with no belongings. I wandered the streets a couple hours. Somehow, I found myself walking through some sort of mirror and glass store. No matter where I turned in this store, mirrors were all over the walls, my own image was reflected back to me from a thousand sides, what looked like doorways into other rooms were only large mirrors. What was worse, there were others here to, wandering the mirrors just as I was. What were they doing here? Why was it so crowded? Was this a party? But no: I saw a cashier, price tags…what was this place, why had I come in here? I think I had come in to look for a phone, but I saw no phone I was allowed to use. The more I wandered those mirrors, the more terrified I became.

I fled that store, whatever it was, and went straight back to Cleo Wallace. "I want my medication," I told Stuart, "and then I'm leaving again." "You can't have it both ways," said Stuart, "if you leave you can't have your medication."

I stayed, and within a few days I had signed some legal papers I did not understand. I don't know what they were: all I knew was now if I wanted to leave, I would have to escape again. This was easier than being let go: the truth was if I ever made it away, I would only go right back.

78

I just remembered a dream. It wasn't a dream I had before waking an hour ago. I must have had it recently, though. I was just pouring some Turkish coffee in my kitchen when the dream image came to my mind. Perhaps it's not even a dream; perhaps it's something I saw on TV. It is one of those memories one has that one cannot place, an image that I saw at some point, whose origin and circumstances I have completely forgotten, and yet I remember it perfectly. I am looking at a newborn baby, and the doctors are coming to circumcise him. I am terrified for the baby. Then, it is over as quickly as it began, and the baby doesn't seem in the least disturbed.

One of my roommates in LA, whom I met in a hospital there, had obsessive compulsive disorder. When he was a little baby, his father was mentally unstable, and held a razor up to his cheek. I don't remember if the razor actually cut him at all. I don't think it did. This roommate always told me this story, and apparently it had had a profound effect on him as an adult. He wasn't one of these people who become righteous victims of abuse and blame their parents for everything. He would just tell me the story again and again, as it distressed him very much. He didn't ever call it "child abuse". In my mind, I always thought, "I wonder what effect his circumcision had on him." He was Jewish; but I was circumcised just like he, and I'm not Jewish. I could never see why his father holding a razor up to his cheek as a baby would distress him so much now. Or, if it did, why his circumcision did not. Perhaps I'm just being cold. My father, after all, never held a razor up to my cheek; how am I to know what it's like?

I just kind of nodded whenever he told me the story. I'd heard much worse before.

79

A young boy at puberty very quickly learns a distinction between private life and public life. He is consumed with sexual fantasies in private, which he would be ridiculed and humiliated for if he made them public. He masturbates, he suspects and sometimes knows all his friends do as well—but he also knows it is understood by all that no one is to admit to it publicly, and everyone is to do it only in private, and deny it in public. Thus he learns the contradictions between private life and public life, and he lives these contradictions and grows up believing in them.

With me, I went too far. I placed all sexual desire into the sphere of "private life". I remember thinking about dating—this institution of dating everyone found so naturally normal and public. I said to myself, "But it's only set up for sex—a completely private thing. How is it that we can speak so plainly and openly about dating?—it's all about the private life of sex after all." I even, later on, after I was schizophrenic, would sometimes look at fully dressed women on the street and say to myself, "But I can see, plain as day, their bulging breasts. True, they have clothes over them—but I can still see bulging breasts, in public for anyone to notice—breasts are a thoroughly sexual and private thing, after all—this is all so obscene." But then I consoled myself that there was no way for the women to hide the bulges of their breasts, unless they pressed them down painfully with some sort of girdle; so I assumed that it was only by absolute necessity that the bulges were public at all.

Thus, from the beginning, I have been ashamed of expressing any sexual desire in public. I never dated in high school—I had a few flings, but I never followed up on them. I was always shy to make the first move, except when I was 14 and determined to lose my virginity once and for all. After that, more and more I grew so ashamed of kissing a girl, asking a girl out, or making any type of public advance, that I have never had a steady relationship in my life. To ask a girl out was public after all—it was public expression of sexual desire, something I have always been naturally ashamed of. While the other boys in high school could admit to finding girls attractive in very explicit terms, I was ashamed to do so.

This putting of obscene sexual desire into the private sphere is something we all do. We would be very offended, after all, if we heard a particular obscene sex act described on broadcast TV, even if it was one we fantasized about in private. We very naturally do not discuss such fantasies at a dinner with friends, and would sometimes even deny having them in public with certain people. But with me, such a distinction was not so easy to draw the line on—where exactly do I draw the line here?—I ended up drawing in on almost any hint of sexual desire, and stuffed all that into my little box of "private life". Most people naturally, unconsciously, are able to draw that line in a healthier way. I knew I would get around to schizophrenic neurosis about sex eventually.

80

In the apartment in Los Angeles where I lived with various roommates that moved in and moved out over 5 years, I had one roommate named Timothy who was a schizophrenic and addicted to cigarettes. I did not smoke in those days, and I was a vegetarian who basically ate a normal American high-fat, potato chip and French fries diet, minus the meat. But I was very fit, and was constantly lifting weights, running, and riding my bike around town. I used to weigh my camping backpack down with about 40 pounds of water bottles and dumbbells, and go jogging for two or three miles wearing it.

Anyway, I was a paranoid wreck mentally, on very high doses of Loxapine and Lithium. But I never talked about or acted on my delusions, and though I showed up to school without having showered, wearing dirty clothes, and psychotic, I was able to do all right with a full load most semesters at Santa Monica College. In fact, I credited my obsession with studying for school with keeping me healthy; it gave me something to obsess about, so I wouldn't be left just to sit and think, and kept me busy 24 hours a day. Timothy, on the other hand, had nothing to do with his time; he never went to college that I know of, he wasn't working and his parents were paying all his bills, and so he, basically, needed something to occupy himself with. Schizophrenics, though being almost always too disabled to work, and usually not very social, need something to do with their days just like everyone, after all. Timothy found this in speed. There was a drug dealer living in our building, and Timothy was always down in his apartment. Sometimes Timothy would invite this drug dealer's other clients into our apartment, who would show up desperately needing a hit of something, to use our phone and beep the dealer when he was out.

Timothy knew when he moved in that he was only allowed to smoke in his room, and on the balcony. One day, he stood just inside from the balcony, and lit up a cigarette. I said to him, "You're not allowed to smoke in here, you have to go out onto the balcony." He stood there doing something at the table, and said he would be out in just a second. But I insisted. I was very firm about it. I demanded that he go out on the balcony immediately.

I didn't realize how ridiculous this was at the time. Here we were, in an apartment with a carpet stained beyond repair, papers and trash all about the living room floor because I was too lazy to get a wastepaper basket for my computer desk. The cockroaches so infested our apartment that I didn't bother killing the ones who crawled across me as I slept, it happened so much; I only threw them across the room and rolled over in my sleeping bag on the floor. Dishes were piled up in the sink; the kitchen floor went without sweeping for months. Timothy was strung out on speed, and I didn't object if he invited some strung out, pale, skin and bones white woman in to come and beep the dealer.

More than that, we were both psychotics in a bad way at the moment, which we mostly kept to ourselves, though I would hear Timothy constantly talking to himself all night. And here I was, as strict about smoking in the apartment as my mother would be. It was so absurd of me! I can't imagine what he thought.

81

Back at Cleo Wallace, I spent most of my free time reading and writing. From the time when I was first off RAP in the lockdown unit, the staff provided loose-leaf paper for me, and I wrote. My first work was a rambling account of my first psychotic break, told in the third person with my name changed, and the characters of my friends swapped about—I described Frederick just as I saw Leo, etc. Most of it was an account of what I had seen on LSD, creative visualization masterpieces described in agonizing detail, my inner world I had created in my shamanic visualization journeys into the underworld, the spirits I had communed with and the complex system their personalities formed in my life, and other such subjective fantasies and dreams. Very little of it described actual interaction with other people or any characters. Much of it was detailed, gory, disturbing descriptions of all sorts of torture and violence; I had decided, in the vision I had of the great work I would create, to exchange the disturbing sexual imagery that plagued me with disturbing violent imagery. To the death metal fan, there is nothing shameful about disturbing violence in prose, after all.

This work ended not with the protagonist's entry into a hospital, but his suicide. There was nothing in it about being admitted to a hospital, the psychosis ever ending, or even any suggestion that it was, after all, psychosis he was in the grip of. He wasn't schizophrenic. He was what I thought I was before I was admitted to the hospital. The manuscript, when I finished it, was I think a little under 200 handwritten pages. I still have it somewhere, but the manuscript is not important enough to me to make any copies of it, even for its safety.

After this, I wrote purely imagined short stories, the content of which was mainly nonsensical and imaginative, though they were about characters and had a plot to them. I have forgotten really what they were about, and many of them have been lost, though I think I still have a few in the form of handwritten pages sitting in my closet somewhere.

Incidentally, I typed two or three of my best stories onto my father's computer while on pass and gave I think two to my friend Brad, who was still in high school. Brad and I had sort of drifted apart as early as our freshman year, since he was one grade lower than me, though I remained good friends with his older brother, Ramsey. Brad told me when I saw him in 1996 that he had plagiarized one of those stories I sent him in 1991, turning in the whole story just reworked a little, to his high school creative writing teacher as an assignment. "What could I do?" he told me. "The assignment was overdue and I had nothing." He said the teacher liked it so much he gave him a B even though it was two weeks late. The teacher even said to him, "If I didn't know better, I would say you couldn't have written that." But the teacher had liked it, he said, which I took as a compliment. I didn't give a damn that he had plagiarized me; I was flattered.

I remember one time in the quiet room, walking a circle through the square made by the white, cinderblock walls, thinking up a story. There was a phrase in my mind, "It feeds on your sorrow," and I began to think, "What is it that feeds on your sorrow? What is it?" and I imagined some monster that lived at the bottom of a lake, no, that *was* the lake…soon, I had it all figured out.

What was I reading at the time? They wouldn't let me read the Clive Barker and Stephen King I wanted to read—all my books had to be approved. I don't remember all I read, all that I was allowed to read, but I do remember three books in particular. *Tales of Mystery and Imagination,* which was a collection of stories by Edgar Allan Poe (incidentally, they required that I make a paper cover for the book, because of the frightening picture of a skeleton or something on the cover); *Quantum Questions*, which was a collection of essays by Einstein, Heisenberg, Sir Arthur Eddington, and other 20th century physicists (I still have it, and am presently referring to it for name spellings as I write); and *The Essential Descartes*, a collection of Descartes's most important philosophical writings. I was, at the time, an outsider artist when it came to fiction, and not a very good one.

There was an ongoing inside joke between mainly Mike and Stuart, with whom I became friendly even after being taken down by them, that went like this: "They just don't understand." This came from the movie *A Fish Called Wanda,* from the scene in which the pseudo-intellectual played by Kevin Klein, after being called an ape by the character played by Jamie Lee Curtis, says, "Apes don't read Nietzsche." "Yes they do," she says; "they just don't understand." Whenever they saw me reading *Quantum Questions* or that collection by Descartes, they would say, "They just don't understand," and yuck it up between them. But alas, they were right: I didn't understand a word of those books. I'd had only the education of a high school student at the end of his sophomore year, and I hadn't been applying myself in school since the sixth grade. I remember asking if anyone knew what "ontological" meant, as it wasn't in the dictionary. "Look up 'onto', and then look up 'logical'," one mental health worker suggested. No one knew what it meant any more than I did.

Thus I passed my time at Cleo Wallace, reading and writing. The school at Cleo Wallace was a complete joke. We would go and sit in these buildings and do different absurd little activities, but usually we merely sat there and read whatever we felt like, or, as in my case, wrote. There was a quiet room in the school, and the teachers were too busy sitting out students for acting up or watching them sit in the corner of the quiet room, so there was no real education.

When I discussed wanting to move into my own apartment one time with my therapist at Cleo Wallace, she said, "What about school?" "I don't think I'll go," I said. "You're going to drop out of school?" she said. "I'll study for my GED," I said. "Call a spade a spade," she said; "that's dropping out of school." I ought to have told her, "If you want to call a spade a spade, I already have dropped out."

There was one thin, bearded teacher at Cleo Wallace who saw me reading philosophy. "That's what I studied in college," he said. He gave me a book by Whitehead, of which I could not comprehend a word. When I told him I couldn't make sense of it, he leant me a book called *A Concise Introduction to Philosophy*, which had no original work of any major philosopher; it was by a contemporary professor less with something original to say and more with a talent for writing clearly. I devoured this book, and I think I actually understood most of it. This book was the reason why, when asked on a form what my major was at Santa Monica College, I wrote "philosophy", and I have never changed my mind since.

82

After I had been in the lockdown unit of Cleo Wallace perhaps two months, and had become obedient, I was transferred back to Unit E. Before I was to go there, I was to have a meeting with Bill and Mike (Mike was the one who had pulled my hair to force me to sit up). I had filled out a patient's rights form about this, which were made available to the patients on demand (though I don't know where they went once you turned them in). I had received a reply saying, basically, that I was right: Mike had not done the physical management according to procedure. So I was to meet with Bill and Mike so that Mike could apologize, and assure me that it wouldn't happen again at Unit E, where I was going, and where he still worked.

Mike basically said, very sincerely, "I was wrong, and, I am sorry." He didn't say it like it was a small matter for him to apologize: it was for him a weighty thing to say one is sorry, and so he was doing it without defending himself or making excuses: he was sorry. Had I known Mike better, I would have known how difficult, or at least unusual, this must have been for him. He never admitted he was wrong unless he knew, beyond doubt, that he had actually acted inappropriately, and had no viable excuse. Though he did other things less severe for which I demanded an apology later, he never gave me another one.

But I didn't know him very well at the time of this meeting. I said to him, "At the time of the incident, you were doing anything to me you wanted; you had the power to do it, and there was no one to stop you. That's not something I can forgive." I think he learned later, in my friendship with him, that this was only an angry jab, it was only I getting all the meager revenge that I could; and that within a few months I had forgiven him, and could even look up to him, though I never told him I had forgiven anything.

83

Though I ran away several times again once I was readmitted to Unit E, at some point I saw the futility of this and actually played their game, obeyed all the rules, and moved up the levels. I went from a room with three others in the bunks, to one with a single bunk bed, one for me, and one for the child molester who slept above me. I was friends with the child molesters, and though all of us often taunted them as "baby rapers", most of us got along with them all right. The one I was sharing a room with was especially well thought of by the staff. He was "working on his issues", he was obedient to everyone, he was in the middle of an honest and determined attempt at changing his ways. He told me when I first roomed with him, "You can never undress with me in the room; always tell me to go outside, then get in bed, and tell me when I can come in." I often forgot this rule, or didn't see it as particularly pressing; but whenever I began to undress at night with him in the room he would get frantic and say: "Stop! That's not allowed!" He would not allow himself the slightest temptation, and I have great respect for that even now. Soon enough, he was discharged to his own apartment, and I have no idea what ever became of him after that.

Then I went from this level to the highest levels, the levels whose members got to sleep in the basement, where no sexual perpetrators were allowed. I remember going on a day trip to get ice cream with the staff; only the high levels were allowed such privileges. I also remember not only going on pass, but taking the bus on pass all the way to see my mother in Aurora, and again taking the bus back to Cleo Wallace. Whenever I was sat out now, I complied right away, terrified that even the sit-out would jeopardize my status. The problem with this, though, was that, when I was finally released, it did not prepare me in any way to live at my father's house. When I was released that summer of 1990, and expected to take the city bus 50 miles to Cleo Wallace every day for day treatment, with complete freedom and responsibility, I was totally unprepared. I refused to go to day treatment some days; other days I spent day treatment (which was only showing up to that absurd Cleo Wallace school) disobeying the teachers and going to the quiet room. I knew they did not have the same power over me anymore; I could wait out the day in the quiet room, and around four o'clock they had to let me go to catch my bus home. I remember walking into an AA meeting in Denver they insisted I attend, and suddenly feeling like everyone could hear my thoughts again; I was falling apart.

After less than two weeks of this, I found myself readmitted to Unit E. This time I was angry. I had gained my freedom only to see it all crumble beneath me once more. I lay in bed and wept. I would not obey them any more.

84

From shortly after my 18th birthday on September 7th, until the time I was discharged to a hospital in Los Angeles in February or March of the next year, I was held in the lockdown unit. I had given up on them and they had given up on me. I had been a long time obsessed with a female mental health worker at Unit E, and now I was threatening to kill her. My therapist did not constantly tell me anymore, "Just follow the rules, play it our way, and you'll be discharged." Rather, we would meet, and she would say, "It doesn't sound like the medication is working; I'll have your doctor up your dose." I do not know my exact dose. All I remember is taking several of the green hexagonal Haldol pills that were either 20 or 25 milligrams each in the morning, and several more in the evening. I could not sit through a community meeting with my eyes open, though they tried to force me to, sitting me out if I closed them. I had absolutely no emotion. The powerful medication took all creativity and feeling from me. I wandered about like a zombie, my only creative acts the escape attempts I would every few weeks commit myself to.

It's funny, now that I think about it, but I think I could have easily escaped. There were two back doors to the dayroom, two magnetically locked doors that led to hallways, which led to doors to the outside. I remember the other patients telling me when they had managed to stage a riot while I was gone several had escaped by kicking the magnetically locked doors as hard as they could, which burst open. I even remember a mental health worker telling me, "If you put a short fence around a dog all his life, when he grows bigger, it would be so easy for him to jump the fence; but he won't ever try it, because he believes the fence keeps him in." This mental health worker was an obese, bearded, uneducated man who wore tie-dye and Grateful Dead shirts all the time. He thought it was hilarious that I never simply kicked open those doors just because I believed it was impossible. But still, I never tried to escape by kicking open those magnetically locked doors.

I did try to scale the fence in the yard and twice I got up into the ceiling, holding onto the tops of the cinderblock walls that ended just above the ceiling tiles; but I was always seen and pulled down. There was a telephone station right next to a set of plastic lockers in the day-room. Once, I quickly climbed on top of the telephone station, which allowed me to get on up to the lockers, which allowed me to reach through the ceiling tiles and pull myself up, gripping the top of the cinderblock wall. I did this in the middle of the morning in plain view of the staff; had I really wanted to escape, I probably would have done it at night, when they wouldn't have seen me so quickly. As soon as I jumped on top of the telephone station, I heard a nurse say, "Jason! Get down!" As soon as I was on top of the lockers, they realized what I was doing. And when I had my upper body through the ceiling tiles, pulling myself up to get on top of the wall and go right over the doors until I made it into an unsecured area, one or two staff members were already pulling me down by my waist.

Going through the same routine, day in, day out, with no therapy (there was never any psychological therapy at Cleo Wallace), and noth-ing to amuse us, we found ways to find amusement. One day, I was eating lunch with my friends Mark (who gave me the acid tab later on), Erica, and Robin, when I said to them, "Let's tell them to fuck off. All they can do is send us to the quiet room, where we can scream our heads off at them." Erica thought it would be fun; the others weren't so sure. Soon enough, Erica and I stood and yelled things at the staff like, "Fuck you! Fuck you all!" We weren't angry; we were having a good time. We continued to scream at them when they sat us out, so they said, "Go to the quiet room," to both of us. If we refused, the next step would be the staff all crowding around us, saying, "You have three sec-onds to go to the quiet room," and then a physical management and all that. But we weren't out for a bad time; we were out for a good time. We walked right into the quiet rooms. I could hear Erica screaming and having fun, and she could hear me doing the same (the two quiet rooms were right next to each other). We screamed, we sang, we yelled obscenities, we told the staff to go fuck themselves; it was a thoroughly great time. For one brief moment, they had no control over us; we would scream as long as we wanted, we could say whatever we wanted, and there was nothing they could do to control us. It was, at the very least, an amusement.

When we finally decided to calm down and sit in the corner of our quiet rooms, and then do our sit-outs, we were told we each had two days of RAP for "rioting". "I'm glad I didn't do it with you," Mark said to me when my RAP was over.

85

I am thinking of the first lines of the Bible I ever read. I suppose I read a little of it as a child; I remember finding a Bible in the basement of a relative's house while at play, and reading the first lines of Genesis. It was eerie actually; as I read these verses, in the basement alone, I suddenly grew afraid of the power of these "holy words", the occult magic of this "holy book", as if by reading them I would summon spirits or cause some spiritual disaster. This Bible I remember being black and saying simply on the front, "The Holy Bible". I grew frightened and put it back down after reading just a few of the opening verses.

I grew up in a family that was ethnically Christian. But my parents never went to church or discussed anything spiritual with us, and they still do not consider themselves Christians, though they will give presents at Christmas and my mother sends me a cute card every Easter, usually having to do with bunnies or eggs.

But back in the spring of 1992, I was renting that room in a predominantly Muslim area of West Los Angeles (there was a mosque on our block, and the Muslims would pack it every Friday. Several years later, I would be living a couple miles away, and I would begin to attend that Mosque and go through the "declaration of Faith" that served as a conversion ceremony.). I wasn't interested in Islam at the time, though I didn't know a thing about it, and the Muslims always seemed like friendly, peaceful people. (One Friday, just when prayers were over, I was walking down my street and came upon about five large Muslim men walking the other direction. They were wearing traditional Middle Eastern dress, and one of them said to me, through a thick accent, as I approached, "How are you my brother!" He had a wide smile on his face and seemed to be saying with it, "Peace upon you! Peace upon the whole world! The world is such a wonderful place after all, isn't it?").

But back to my first Bible. It was given to me by a Jehovah's Witness as I was doing my laundry in a Laundromat. I began this time at the New Testament; reading the minutiae of the Torah's laws and who begot whom did not interest me. I remember reading and not understanding very much of it, and yet finding it interesting. I remember reading about the centurion who said to Jesus "I too have men under me, and I say to one, 'Go,' and he goes..." meaning that if Jesus will only give the command, the centurion's servant will be healed. I pondered over these words of the centurion, wondering what on earth they could mean. Now, at least, I understand that part; but I still have trouble with phrases of Jesus like, "The eye is the lamp of the body; when the eye is healthy, the whole body is filled with light; but when the light in you is darkness, how great is that darkness!" What does this mean? I have no idea.

Nonetheless, I was struck by Jesus's absolute willingness to sacrifice everything for the sake of the good. I too wanted to sacrifice every comfort and pleasure for the sake of good; I had wanted to be Gandhi at Cleo Wallace, and now I was given a chance to actually express my pure, saintly love for all of humankind. I bought homeless men lunches often; I ate a bland diet to save money for charity. I remember writing letters home to people who were only friends, and writing "I love you," at the end, as a way of expressing my unconditional love for every man, woman, and child on the earth. If this caused me embarrassment, or if I felt embarrassed to write it, I purposefully sacrificed this feeling for the sake of love, and went ahead and wrote it.

This was when I first began attending the Seventh-Day Adventist Church. But why did I choose that particular church? The answer lies in some very strange conversations I'd had with Mike at Cleo Wallace.

86

One day, back at Unit E, while I was playing video games with the other boys and Mike, the subject of concentration camps came up in our conversation. Mike said something like, "That is going to happen, right here, in the US, very soon." He was perfectly serious. I argued the point with him, saying, "The Supreme Court wouldn't allow it; we have free speech here; we can say anything." "Can we burn a flag?" said Mike. I didn't at the time know you could burn a flag; all I knew was the recent controversy when the Supreme Court had struck down a law that prohibited it. I ought to have said to him: "Sure we can," but I didn't know we could; neither did Mike, probably, though he would have had he followed the news a little more closely.

Mike and I used to go on long walks in which he explained to me that years earlier he'd had an experience of God that told him he knew, just as he knew he existed, that there was a God. This wasn't a mystical "oneness with God" but a humbling experience that told him there was a personal God separate from him, the God of Abraham, Isaac, and Jacob. He told me the political religious right, President Reagan, the (then) President Bush, and many top government officials, were in the middle of a grand conspiracy to overthrow the Constitution, institute military law, and throw everyone who wasn't a Christian into the ovens. "Are there documents relating to this conspiracy?" I asked him

once. "Yes," he said, "I'm sure there are." He didn't, however, offer to
show me any copies of them.

Once, we were talking about outer space aliens. "I know they're
here," he said to me. "How do you know?" I asked. "I'm in contact
with them," he said. He was the type of mysterious, sane, wise and
powerful man who, when he said such things, made you think there
was much he wasn't telling you, and made you believe the little he
actually did. Slowly, I began to believe him. For some reason, I never
told my therapist the content of the discussions; probably I unconsciously knew that if I did, she would put a stop to our walks and conversations.

When Mike first told me the whole story, I began to inflate my own
importance in the little scheme. He said he had been let in on the
secret plans of the government by someone he had met while in the
military. "I had that experience of God in order to show me I was in
the right place" (he'd been signing up for the military) "because of who
I would meet there. I met my spiritual teacher there." I began to think,
"This spiritual teacher had come to him only because God knew he
would one day come to me; it was all to bring me to my mission, and
certainly I will have a very important place in all this; perhaps I will
save the world." I began to believe this, and I told Mike I thought the
spiritual master had met with him only so he could learn the things he
was teaching me, that I had been all along the real goal of all his spiritual education. "You're probably right," he told me.

One day I said to him, "I won't be able to resist the government
when they torture me; I'm afraid of them, and I don't think I'm strong
enough." "I can tell you're strong enough," he said, "I could see it in
you that time when you first got here, when I managed you."

Thus did my mission grow inside of me. I did not think about it a
whole hell of a lot once I was chock-full of Haldol for my last six
months or so at the lockdown unit. But once I was free, it came back to
me, and I began to believe in it again. This was the time of the Gulf
War when Bush had said all those things about the "new world order"

that sent so many people into paranoia. I too found what he said frightening, though I didn't know about the others who were frightened of it. I even cut out newspaper articles that had the more frightening lines of Bush's speeches, and sometimes quoted them in my fiction. I wished oftentimes I still had Mike around, so that I could really prepare for this "new world order" he had warned me would come to pass, even before Bush had made those speeches. But there was no Mike here in LA.

I recalled a conversation with Mike in which I had asked him if there were others who believed as he did. "The Seventh-Day Adventists," he said. "Seventh Day at Venice?" I said. "Yes," he said. I didn't know what an Adventist was or what was important about a seventh day; I knew Venice was a place in Italy that perhaps had something to do with the Bible or something. So when I was on my own in Los Angeles I looked through the white pages for "Seventh Day at Venice," and found no listing for that. I did see, however, "Seventh-Day Adventist Church," and I thought, "Sounds like it to me."

87

When I think of where Mike is now, I find it somewhat humorous. From what he firmly believed back in 1990, it was a matter of a few years before the government started putting him and all the other true Christians into the ovens, under the flag of false Christianity. If Mike still believes the same things now, he is into his mid- to late-40s, still preparing for the same thing, probably saying to himself, "Any day now, any day now it will happen." He is growing frailer; that body he had put into top form and shape in his 30s in order to prepare for the trauma it would experience in those camps is starting to get a little harder to keep so strong; perhaps he suffers aches and pains or arthritis. Such a strong belief as his, which formed his whole reason for all his life activities, twelve years later when it still hasn't happened, becomes something in between hilarious and sad. But certainly were he to read this, he would think I am the faithless fool mocking him just like the crowds foolishly mocked Jesus; it's hard to argue with such people when they categorize you in such a way.

As for me, I began going to the Seventh-Day Adventist Church of Santa Monica. Though I had briefly gone to the closer Seventh-Day Adventist Reform Movement Church, which had a small, very radical and cult-like congregation, I felt more at home in a more mainstream environment. The end times were discussed so little in the Santa Monica church that I began to forget about it again, and replace it with my simple saint complex; I was utterly devoted, even psychotically, to God and the good.

I remember in my meetings with the pastor, Pastor Dahl, coming to him with questions such as, "Is it wrong to look at a *Playboy* magazine?" I was so careful I wouldn't even look at underwear ads. Pastor Dahl told me he himself used to have a *Playboy* subscription, and saw nothing wrong with it; we argued over the issue at length. He did not yet know I was schizophrenic and saw how devoted and pious I was; one day when I showed up for our scheduled meeting he introduced me to his daughter, who was a beautiful blond young woman. "You are in your second year at Santa Monica College?" said Pastor Dahl. "You and my daughter have a lot in common; she's a junior." Somehow I thought he meant she was a junior in high school; she looked that young; I'm not really sure what exactly he meant. I found her very attractive, but I treated her with such respect that I pretty much ignored her, ashamed to engage her in conversation and thus be hitting on the pastor's daughter.

In my first meeting with the pastor, he offered me some raw, juicy figs. At first I refused, thinking that this was probably a cult and he was trying to drug me; but then I ignored my paranoia, as I have learned to in society, and ate two of them. The inside of them was full of seeds. I did not eat the seeds. I had never eaten or seen raw figs, and I found them delicious. The pastor said, "I see you like those. Figs aren't exactly my favorite fruit myself." I knew right away that the figs were a test: he was testing to see if I was a reincarnated early saint, Paul or James or someone, as the saints will be resurrected first in the end times. If I knew how to eat the figs, and stop at the seeds; if I enjoyed them and liked their taste, this was because I was an Israelite from the time of Jesus, who would enjoy and know how to eat raw figs. I did not tell him these ideas, though, but went on eagerly learning everything he taught me about the Bible.

But, as the months of going to this church went by, in my mind was a belief that this was a cult that would abduct and brainwash me at any moment. One day, we had a potluck after church. A young woman named Gina gave me a cup of fruit juice; certainly there were drugs in it. I drank one cup, then the next she gave me. This was it. I would pass out from the drug, and the next thing I would know I would be ready for programming in a cabin somewhere in the mountains or desert. There was a woman speaking before the crowd, in front of the tables, about some sort of trip she went on with the church, some sort of camp or something. Was this my first introduction to where I was going? Was she saying to me, "It's all right: we'll take care of you where you're going; they took me too, and here I am to tell you my story"? Was the purpose of this whole potluck to drug me and take me off to be programmed?

I had to escape. I stood and tried to walk behind my neighbor away from the tables, then fell into some metal foldout chairs and knocked them to the floor. The woman in front stopped her speech, and everyone looked at me. "Sorry!" I said, and I ran out the door without setting the chairs back up. I was already dizzy from the drug; I had to escape before I passed out.

An hour and a half later, I had made it home, and I still hadn't passed out. But certainly it was only because I hadn't been given a strong enough dose of the drug. Those Seventh-Day Adventists would be coming to my door to kidnap me at any moment.

A few months later, once this psychosis had been replaced by one only more paranoid, new neighbors moved in next door to my apartment. I would later learn they were a young Israeli couple; but at the time, whenever I heard them outside, I said, "There they are—those Seventh-Day Adventists who are spying on me. They even moved in right next to me."

88

Before I was old enough to be off my father's insurance, Aetna had paid, I believe, something over a quarter-million dollars for my treatment. It's amazing to me that they continued to pay hundreds of dollars a day at Cleo Wallace, after my therapist had given up on making me functional there, and I was only being held because they did not know what else to do with me. This was the case for my last three to five months at Cleo Wallace. Finally, the insurance company stepped in. I would be moved to a hospital in California. That was the only option they would accept.

But I was still there under a committal, which said I was "gravely disabled"; thus they could keep me against my will. My doctor, whom I only rarely saw, sat down with me and told me they could not force me to go to the hospital in Los Angeles. There was no such thing, he said, as a non-consensual transferal from one institution to another, especially from one state to another. At first, I thought this was great: they couldn't force me to go, so I refused. Then the insurance company said if I refused I would go to a board-and-care home, one of those very low-budget places where the mentally ill who have no other options spend their lives and grow old. But the option of going to California was still open to me. All my family was not ready to give up on me, and pressured me to agree to the California hospital. I hadn't had much good experience with hospitals, and I had no idea what this California one was like. But in the end I agreed to try it, and it turned out to be the right decision.

A couple of months later, my dose of Haldol was lowered so I could at least get on an airplane with my father (the Haldol itself was enough to render anyone dysfunctional), and I was discharged from Cleo Wallace for the last time. Since then, I have often wanted to run into one of those mental health workers in my neighborhood here in Denver, just to speak with him as an equal, just to be on equal footing with one of them rather than the way it was then, with all the power on their side. It would be fun, I think, just to see one of them on the street somewhere, and approach and speak with him, and see the look in his eyes that would say, "I had better not say anything to him like I would have said years ago." I wouldn't do anything violent or cruel to him; I would only enjoy watching him see that now he doesn't have any power over me, watch him realize that we are now equals and I have perfect freedom, just like him. Then I would probably buy him a beer, and we would talk about old times.

89

My therapist at A Touch of Care in West Los Angeles often told the story, to me or to my family when they came to see me, of the hospital staff's reaction to me when I first arrived. "We had been told by the people at Cleo Wallace that he was a very chronic and grave case, that he was dangerous, that he was threatening people, that unless there were a miracle, he would end up in state hospitals for the rest of his life. And then along comes this pussycat, completely friendly, honest, and shy—a harmless creature!" This was an adult institution, not one that treated delinquents and criminals; the schizophrenics there, if they were chronic cases, were merely withdrawn and could not be reasoned with, did not respond to medication. But I could carry on a conversation with my therapist, give people comforting advice during group therapy, and I was trying to make friends with the other—I want to say "patients", but we were referred to here as "clients".

The others, I think, liked me well enough in the beginning. But my social skills had much wanting. Whenever I met someone new there, I said, "How long have you lived in California?" When they said, "All my life" or "12 years," or whatever they said, I would wait for them to finish, and then say, "How many earthquakes have you been in?" I repeated this question to everyone; but everyone in Los Angeles takes it for granted that there will be tremors and occasionally larger quakes, and no one really thinks about it as much as I imagined they did. I remember after having lived there five and a half years, I was drinking one night in my apartment and the apartment suddenly trembled a little. "Is that an earthquake?" my roommate said, suddenly nervous. "Just a little shaking!" I said. "If it shakes again it'll be just a little ride for us—come on, shake again, give me some fun!" I was drunk; I wasn't afraid of the shaking anymore.

But this hospital in LA was a rest I sorely needed. I got to sleep in weekends as late as I wanted. I had a therapist whom I had long sessions with and to whom I could unload all my worries and emotions. I did not have any therapy at Cleo Wallace, and I did not trust my therapist there to tell her anything of what went on inside of me; she had been the enemy there. But here there was no enemy. I was not at A Touch of Care involuntarily; I could have left anytime I wanted, but there was no reason to leave. As soon as I was functional enough, they would help me find my own place somewhere in LA; there was no need to rush it. This place was like a much-needed vacation from the stress Cleo Wallace had put me under.

Over the next 9 months, the Touch of Care therapists and staff began to prepare me, in concrete ways, for living in my own place, paying my own rent, getting my GED and going to college. Now I did not have a single irrational goal—escape—rather, I had the much more complex problem of learning to live life with my illness. This was a more difficult task, but I had a lot of help along the way.

90

I am trying to think of what led me to first put on a dress. I think it was that all-female therapy group I went to every week. One day, Jay-Marie invited me to join it, saying, "Come along to our group tonight—it'll be fun." So I began going to this all-female therapy group in which we got in touch with things feminine—I included. I was already feminine enough: I was 6'2.5" tall and weighed just under 170 pounds—I was very thin. I was also very much into being the sympathetic, loving Gandhi of group therapy, never blaming anyone, always being a shoulder to cry on. I was full of love and hope and determined to help everyone I could; no harsh words or anger ever passed my lips. I was a big hit in the all-female therapy group.

But the dress. It began with a skirt. One night I remember thinking...a skirt is just a different shape of cloth than pants...it is completely arbitrary to call one "masculine" and the other "feminine"; they are only different shapes, and we impose these categories onto them according to purely arbitrary processes...ought I to let society force me never to wear a skirt because of such arbitrary, meaningless categories? Of course not! There you have it: and then next day I bought a long-hemmed, cheap black skirt at a second-hand clothes store at Venice Beach.

Then one night I was with my father in Santa Monica, wearing my skirt, and I saw a dress in some store that wasn't frilly or feminine, but very plain and modest. It had dark tan and beige coloring, and a hem that would go down to my ankles. It was my birthday, and my father had asked me what I wanted. "I want that," I said, pointing at the dress. He bought it for me, and I began to wear it on the outings we made on weekends at A Touch of Care.

Once, when walking through the Westside Pavilion in my dress, two gay men were sitting on a bench, and saw me go by. One of them looked me up and down, and made a long, drawn out wolf whistle. I was very uncomfortable at this; it hadn't occurred to me that I would be thought of as gay. But I went on wearing my dress, and didn't seem to think it was that unusual. When I would a few years later be dating a woman I met at school, I would say to her at some point that I used to wear a dress, and then say, "Do you think that's weird?" "Yes," she would say; "I do."

An even more difficult question than "Why did I begin wearing the dress?" is "Why did I stop wearing the dress?" I think most cross-dressers get a desire to wear women's clothes that is ongoing. On the other hand, after I was discharged from A Touch of Care, I still had my dress hanging up in my closet, but I sort of forgot it was there, and never wore it. Then, in the fall of 1992 when I was in the middle of a brief fling with a bipolar woman named Russia, I gave her the dress, and have never felt like wearing one since. I guess I have decided that, yes, to call one shape of cloth feminine is completely arbitrary, but I wouldn't go to another culture and start doing things that offend them, even if such norms are arbitrary. Why should I offend my own culture, then?

Before giving the dress to Russia, I put it on so she could see. She pretended to think it was awfully hip that I used to wear a dress. "Wow," she said, "I don't know any men who wear dresses—that's so cool." But she didn't complain when I gave her my only dress, and when she broke it off with me she didn't return it. Now, since I weigh around 212 pounds, and sometimes grow a great bushy beard, I don't think it would look very good on me anyway.

91

Once, I had shown up to an anthropology class at SMC completely certain everyone around me could hear my thoughts. I was on high doses of Loxapine at the time, but this only succeeded in making my personality very subdued and numb. As I was staring at the professor as she lectured about a group of people she had studied in Nigeria, our eyes met just when I was creatively imagining some visualization picture-show for the class. She lost her train of thought for a second, looking at a pair of eyes that did not see what was outside, but were merely staring into space as the mind was seeing something internal. Her eyes widened for a second, until we looked away from each other, and then she went on with her lecture.

The next class I took of hers, she handed out forms in the beginning in which she asked for our names, phone numbers, and majors. There was a space on the form that said, "This space is for anything you might want to add that I should be aware of during the semester." I didn't write anything there. I thought to myself, "She asked that question on the form because of me: she's trying to gather some information those English professors can use against me." (I thought a group of English professors were plotting against me.)

92

As I write this, it has been 20 days since I began the rough draft of this manuscript. I generally don't edit a manuscript until I am finished with the first draft, but there have been sections here and there I have deleted already. My life during the writing of this manuscript: I wake up at 9:00 or 10:00 in the morning, drink a cup of Turkish coffee, smoke some cigarettes, write, drink more Turkish coffee, smoke cigarettes, write another one of these short chapters. I eat a small loaf of white bread or some rice around noon, just so my stomach can handle a pot of tea, then write. I go to McDonald's or 7-11 for something to eat around six o'clock, drink more tea, write. I drink tea, Turkish coffee, smoke cigarettes, and write until 12:00 or 1:00 a.m.

(I have not been writing this manuscript on my manual typewriter, which I used for the first draft of my last two novels. There would be no way to keep up: the pages would build up, and I would not be able to type them into my computer as fast as I write them.)

My new thing is baking my own bread, and mixing and kneading the dough gives me something to do as I take a break from writing, and then I inevitably write as the dough is rising. I've got to stop obsessing on this book, take it easy, get back into the habit of going on walks for exercise. This book is killing me—I'm eating only microwave burritos, white bread, and potato chips.

What's wrong with me? I can't stop thinking, that's what. No matter how many breaks I take, no matter how much I pause and say I'll put this book down, I get a new idea, and have to write it down. It wasn't like this on Haldol; on Haldol I wrote only four pages a day, but Haldol has drawbacks of its own, including that stomach inflammation I have had for years, which is completely better on Loxapine.

This is wearing me out—this is no way to live. When I'm done with this book I'll only get a new idea for another. I am, after all, a psychotic, constantly obsessing on ideas, constantly writing down strange thoughts. Sometimes I say to myself, "I'm done with writing; I've said all I have to say—won't it be nice never to write again, and paint my worthless paintings for the rest of my life?" But I am incapable of doing this. I said I would do it when I finished my last completed novel—then I got an idea for a new novel. I wrote about 90 pages, then got an idea for a completely different philosophical essay. I wrote and finished that, 140 pages after I deleted about 30 more. I haven't yet gone back to my unfinished novel, which I have wanted to get around to, but then 20 days ago I got the idea for this book—this is so maddening. I think I need to change my pills and capsules, those lovely pills and capsules that help me relax, that help me sleep, that help me not to think. I need a higher dose, a dose of something different—anything that will help me stop writing. This is getting ridiculous.

And the worst part is that I keep forgetting to make an appointment with my doctor. The outpatient clinic I go to is so understaffed that they won't have an appointment for me, unless I am about to hang myself, until two months after I call to make one. But my mental life is so obsessed on this book, so unable to remember to even brush my teeth and pick the trash up off my floor, that every day I neglect to make that call. This has been the past 20 days. The past 13 years, as you know by now, have been much worse.

93

I first moved into that apartment at 3560 S. Centinela Avenue, in a little neighborhood of West LA called Mar Vista, just a few blocks north up the hill from Venice Boulevard and Centinela, with a schizophrenic woman I had met at A Touch of Care named Trisha. She moved out about a year later, went off north to Santa Barbara to be closer to her family, where, I learned in the single letter I received from her, she ended up back in an institution at least for a while.

She was a schizophrenic whose major symptom was hallucinations. She would go off into a complete hallucinatory world, and when she was in this state in real life she would sit there shaking, unable to communicate, unable to be reached, and sometimes would harm herself as her hallucinations demanded. But when she was taking medication, she was able to carry on a conversation, interact with people normally, and function in her apartment life. She took one or two classes at SMC while she lived there with me, and as I remember it she got all As.

One day, as she was in her room, the phone rang, and I picked it up. It was Trisha's therapist, and she was almost frantic. She thought

Trisha was hallucinating, as she had gotten a call from her, but had been unable to get any sense out of her. I walked into Trisha's room and saw her there, sitting in the corner on the floor, right by the phone. Her eyes did not see what was around her; her hands were going back and forth over her forearms as if she were going through the motions of cutting herself (though she had no razor in them); her whole body was shaking. Her medication was the "miracle drug" Clozapine, and I would learn only later that she had stopped taking it.

I went to the phone next to her and picked it up, then said to her therapist, "She is hallucinating." Her therapist told me to hold her hand and talk to her, to give her some external stimuli and hopefully draw her out of it, while her therapist drove over to our apartment.

At first I only held her hand and said things like, "They're not real; they'll go away," referring to the characters of her hallucinations, which I knew from speaking with her were some sort of occult figures who consistently returned with the same characteristics as they always had. Then I noticed she was hyperventilating. I wanted her to breathe in slow, deep breaths, rather than the quick shallow gasps she was taking. I said to her, "Breathe slowly and deeply and they'll go away." I was sitting right next to her on the floor, just to her right, holding her hand. Her open window was a couple feet from us, and the neighbors often complained whenever she practiced her drums. I wondered what they thought of what I was saying to her now, as all the windows in that building were always open in the summer because of the heat, and one could easily hear even subdued conversations; I was speaking to her now in a loud, clear voice. But I didn't really care.

In response to me, she began to breathe in frantic, quick, but deep breaths. I said to her, "So you can hear me. Now you're breathing deep, but if you breathe slowly too they'll go away." Soon enough, she was breathing slowly and deeply; but not only that, the hallucinations had left her and she was able to talk to me normally. We went out to the balcony and talked, waiting for her therapist to come. We had to wait quite a while.

Then the therapist arrived, and an administrator from A Touch of Care arrived. As I walked by, the therapist whispered to the administrator, "Jason handled it very well." How had I handled it? I had "cast the demons" out of her just as Jesus used to do; it was my miraculous power, brought about by my generosity to the homeless and my kindness to everyone; saints like I, after all, sometimes gained certain miraculous powers. I did not tell anyone these thoughts. I believed Trisha's therapist was thinking the same thing (did she not seem very amazed that Trisha was back in her right mind when she arrived?); I believed she was only afraid to tell me (did she not merely whisper it to the administrator, instead of tell me directly?). She merely didn't want to tell me I was a miracle-worker, a holy man with holy, magical powers. Though she believed it, who ever heard of a respectable therapist telling a schizophrenic he has magical powers?

While Trisha went back on her medication and back to concerns of her own, while the incident became for her only one hallucination out of hundreds she had dealt with all her life, for me the incident became a precursor to my mission. Perhaps I was not only a saint, perhaps I was a prophet or messiah. I went on denying myself chocolate bars just so I would have 65 cents more to give to the homeless. I went on carrying hot soup or beans down to Venice Boulevard and Centinela every Sunday morning to the homeless people who usually appreciated it. My whole live spread out ahead of me, frightening me—certainly one day I would be a very important spiritual leader with a very important mission.

94

If I write as a psychotic symptom now, it is a new symptom; I was not obsessed with writing the six years I lived in LA. True, I saw myself as a writer; true, I wrote a volume of very sentimental, rhyming poetry and some very bad short stories and a couple bad novellas. But I did not write every day, or even every week. I knew I wanted to be a writer, and even went on a submission campaign before I had any mature work to submit, or knew anything about what was being published. But soon enough, I gave up on submitting to magazines, gave up on trying to get my book of poems published, and put all of my dreams of being a writer into a distant future. I was still very young, and the life ahead of me was still very vast; I may be a writer one day, I thought, but not now. I still hadn't given up on one day becoming the next Gandhi, and that dream wouldn't die until I found my good friends Beer and Cigarettes, and I had given up my daily prayers and extreme devotion to God. Schizophrenics have dreams as young men just like everyone; only they are sometimes, as the case was with me, distorted by psychosis.

Before I started smoking and drinking, when I was going to school full time and in the midst of my extreme piety, I considered, like any good Puritan, leisure time as a sin. This was why I was able to handle a full-time load at SMC and later go full time at UCLA (at least for a year; I never graduated). I was always busy doing some type of work or another, except for the Saturday Sabbath every Seventh-Day Adventist takes more seriously than mainstream Christians take Sunday. Every Friday night just before sundown I would be studying away with my school work, eagerly getting everything done I possibly could, and then from sundown Friday to sundown Saturday I wouldn't do any sort of school work or study, except to read the Bible.

I think my Civil War buff period began with an idea for a sweeping epic fiction taking place during the Civil War, involving outer space aliens, vast conspiracies, and sacred insurgencies. I knew nothing of the Civil War then; I remember when this idea first came to me I asked my therapist, "Was Washington still the Capital during the Civil War? You'd think that would be too close to the South." She didn't know; I didn't know either. So I began to read. I read biographies of major civil war figures; I read histories of the war and book-length accounts of bat-

tles. I started going through that 10-volume biography of Lincoln by
Nicolay and Hay and then gave that up around volume 7. Then I
picked up Carl Sandberg's 6-volume biography of him, and made it
through the first 3.

I'm not sure how much I actually absorbed. I wouldn't let myself
rest and be at leisure, ever, and since I wasn't actually writing this Civil
War epic, I was always reading. (I remember telling one of my professors that, when not signed up for classes, I read an average of something around 170 pages a day.) I also got subscriptions to the Civil
War buff magazines *Civil War Times* and *America's Civil War*, and
devoured every issue of both.

I never wrote that Civil War epic; I tried to start it, and wrote a little
over 100 pages; but I had at the time read very little actual fiction, so
the texture of my style made it sound like a history book. There was
none of the personal detail, the immersion into a world or particular
scene, that is characteristic in good novels. It was all summary and
listed events.

I did, however, write a screenplay that I think was all right, about
John Brown's activities in Kansas during the war before the war, that
period in Kansas history known as "Bleeding Kansas". I think this
screenplay was successful, though not as good as the two screenplays I
have written since; but actually selling a screenplay is more difficult
than getting a book published. I find enough difficulty in just that task;
I think I'll stick to it instead.

I remember once wondering why, if I was really a writer, I actually
wrote so little. I had written much more volume at Cleo Wallace than I
wrote now. Once, I asked myself at the end of 1995, "What did I write
last year?" My answer was, "Well, I wrote my screenplay." That was all
I had written that year, just a screenplay of little more than 100 pages.
I would later, in 1998, write a screenplay of about the same length, and
of much better quality, in two weeks.

It was in the spring of 1996 that I started smoking and drinking. I
had since begun to not be so concerned with the sin of leisure, and the

apartment got filthier, I grew lazier, and I began to just sit and think instead of read all the time. That was also my first quarter at UCLA, when I began to lose interest in school.

One of my roommates at the time, whom I mentioned earlier, named Marty, used to always get on my case about living on disability and being lazy. Marty had a certain innocence about him that came from his poor education. When my other roommate Jim was finally given a job by his stepfather, he said to me, perfectly sincerely, "Maybe I should get a stepfather." His mother was dead.

Marty worked hard at his job stocking shelves in a drugstore, and had worked the same job for over ten years. He had the attitude that I was living on his hard-earned taxes, and got on my case again and again about getting a job. He didn't see any value in going to school; if I were to have any self-respect, I would have to earn my own money. Once I had started smoking and drinking, after over 5 years of being drug and alcohol free, he could see that I was no longer constantly busy, as I had been when I was so devout and pious. "You are never doing things," he said. "You used to always be doing things; now you just smoke cigarettes all the time." I felt bitter toward religion, but somehow I looked back at my former holiness, and felt I had somehow fallen from grace. Sometimes when this feeling was particularly overwhelming I would get on my knees, pray for forgiveness, and tell God I would do my best to get back to how I was before. But I had lost all faith in Christianity. All this talk of "love your neighbor as yourself" had only led me into an extreme self-hatred, as I tried to sacrifice everything for strangers I saw on the street.

Whenever Marty said to me, "You don't do things anymore; you used to always be doing something," it cut deeper than any of his insults in the yelling matches we had. It was pointing to my former sinless life, pointing out how all that had crumbled under me, pointing out that I was now just another man living in sin, subject to addictions, and unable to live in piousness by his very nature. I didn't know what to do about it; but one thing was clear: I was no Gandhi, no saint, and

I had lost a dream of my future when I had lost these illusions of holiness.

95

A question that sometimes occurs to me, and usually gets me into some sort of trouble, is, "What am I going to do for the rest of my life?" That question occurred to me in 1997 after my last completed quarter at UCLA (winter 1997), when I suddenly dropped all courses for the spring quarter, and never went back. I had decided on a humbler future for myself than being a saint and important leader; I would get a job, write in my free time, and begin living the rest of my life. I would be fooling myself to think I would ever be an important philosopher or professor one day (philosophy was still my major), and I needed a realistic goal, and I needed to get on with accomplishing it.

That was the year in which, in a vain effort to cultivate some of my former righteousness, I converted to Islam, and began praying at the mosque in my old neighborhood. When I told one Muslim there I was looking for a job, he promised to make some calls, and eventually found me one. It's amazing what those brothers will do for one another.

The Muslim who found me the job was from some small North African country whose name I didn't recognize at the time, and which I have since forgotten. He drove me to an Islamic center in another part of the city one Ramadan day to break the fast with them. All the way there he told me about the virtues of Islam (he knew I was a recent convert), saying things like, "At any moment you could die. Someone on the street could hit you in the face for no reason, and you could die. It's better not to live like you will never die, and instead prepare for what comes after."

He told me about how, after moving to America, he had fallen away from Islam and had wrecked his car while driving drunk. Now, he was getting married (his future wife was still in some other country), and he felt pressured to go back to living righteously. I have no doubt he honestly believed everything he told me, and was frightened for the state of his own soul, and everything it would go through in hell if he didn't mend his ways. But he had no patience for over-piousness. At a special Ramadan prayer that night at the Islamic center, the imam had sung an entire sura of the Qur'an in Arabic, and it had gone on very long. "That prayer went on too long," he said to me in the car on the way back. "I think I was falling asleep!"

A few days after I had told him I was looking for a job, he called me with two numbers I could call to get an interview. They were both very far away. One lead didn't pan out; the other was the number of a small sporting goods company in the San Gabriel Valley, owned by a Lebanese man named Ibraheem. I called the number and took the bus out there within a week for an interview. I wish Ibraheem had never been interested in hiring me from the start; I'm sure he wishes the same thing.

96

Ibraheem basically ran a small factory, whose employees were all Mexicans (even his wife, who worked there too, was a Mexican American, who had been born in the US), and sold the sports uniforms his factory produced to teen sporting teams and retail stores. When I got to the address for the interview, all I saw was a rundown warehouse with tin siding. There was a little window by the front door, through which I could see a small, empty office; but no one came to the door when I knocked. Could this be the right address? I walked a few blocks away to a payphone, and called Ibraheem's number again. "Just come around back," he told me. I went back to the warehouse and went through the fence to the back door, which was open. Inside there were about three or four Mexicans working away on the sewing machines. Ibraheem invited me to his office, and the interview began.

Ibraheem told me later that he had wanted me for the job as soon as he had seen my resume. He needed someone with some basic education, who knew basic arithmetic and could use a word processor; but he couldn't afford to pay most people with any sort of college education, and offered no insurance or retirement benefits. At the time, though, I was very suspicious of his efforts to get me to work for him. I had been looking around for jobs for a long time, and had gone through many interviews; but I had little work experience, and though I had an associate's degree from SMC I didn't have a bachelor's. My experience was that I was not very marketable, and would have a very hard time getting any job. Why was he so eager to hire me?

I began to suspect that this factory was a sweatshop whose workers were really slaves, and this Ibraheem was going to kidnap me and force me to work at those sewing machines I had seen in the back room. Where did all the clothes in this factory come from? Certainly not from those three or four people I had seen in the back. There was probably another warehouse he would take me to, one surrounded by barbed wire and patrolled by guards, where I would be put to slavery and forced to work the rest of my life merely for food and shelter, held captive there forever. I had seen a recent news story on TV about such a place in LA. It was an apartment building surrounded by barbed wire whose owners had turned it into a clothing factory whose workers had been captive immigrants forced to work as slaves. Apparently this place only got busted once some of the immigrants escaped to tell the police. Was Ibraheem about to drug me and take me to one of these sweatshops? Would I be held captive there, just as I had been at Cleo Wallace?—would I live for months there planning my escape, just as I had done in the not-too-distant past while held captive for my mental illness?

Ibraheem was quite a salesman. Every reservation I had about taking the job he picked apart and tried to convince me it wasn't a concern. He talked on and on; mostly I sat there and listened, lost in my fears. Of course if he offered me a job I ought to take it, I told myself; of course this would be the rational thing for me to do, since I'd had such a hard time finding a job in the past. As the afternoon wore on, Ibraheem talked and talked (he was by nature and profession a salesman, and if you've ever known one, you will know that a salesman can talk). He finally took me out to lunch at a little Middle Eastern restaurant where he often took his clients and associates. He drove me there in his beat up car, and stopped to get gas on the way. In the passenger seat, I glanced over at the gauge to see if he really needed gas. Was he only gassing up for the long drive to the sweatshop? Wasn't this, after all, only a kidnapping?

The waiter at this restaurant knew Ibraheem by name and they spoke in Arabic together. Obviously, the owners of this restaurant were in on it. Ibraheem ordered the shish kabob for me (he thought most Americans liked shish kabob best of all Middle Eastern food), and I don't remember what he got for himself. Normally, I eat very quickly; whenever I go out with my family, I devour my plate before they have taken a few bites. But now I ate slowly. I was worried that the food was drugged. In the back of my mind, I classified this as paranoia, and I had decided long ago never to act on paranoia, but to pretend it wasn't there, so that I could function in school and in society. But it was still a belief of mine. I went ahead and ate the food, but ate it slowly. Ibraheem finished his meal before mine was half-done. I think when we left I still had a good deal of food on my plate.

On the way back to the warehouse, Ibraheem made his offer clear. I would work three days a week to start out, and he would give me $6.50 an hour. The wage was enough. The hours were enough. By this time I was only relieved that he had not, after all, kidnapped me; and I could see we were almost all the way back to where we had started off from. I agreed to take the job. It wasn't, given my mental state at the time, the smartest thing to do.

97

I have been in the habit for years of carrying two wallets: one in my back right pocket, for my cash, and the other in my front left pocket, for my cards and documents. I do this in case I'm robbed on the street: I would give the robber my cash, and wouldn't have to go through the trouble of replacing things like my Medicare card, my ID, and all the important documents I carry. (Just last week, I was going through all these cards, and realized I had been carrying my Social Security card in this wallet for years. There's no reason to carry that around, I thought, and it would be a disaster if it fell into the wrong hands. I put it in a safer place immediately.)

I'm not sure just when I began this two-wallet policy, but I'm sure it began sometime when I was living in LA. I think it began when I would transfer busses around 9:00 at night in downtown Los Angeles, on my way home from work when I worked part time for Ibraheem.

I remember once, when I was carrying only enough cash for my bus fare (it's better, I think, to have a little more than that to give an angry mugger), through the dark streets of downtown, on my way to Venice Boulevard. I don't know if you've ever been to downtown LA, but in the daytime it seems completely different than at night. In the daytime there are office workers, people who work in finance and banking, all sorts of business people on the street. But so far as I could tell from how it looked when a business day was over, none of those people lived downtown. At night, the only people on the streets were scary people.

What I am about to say may sound African American phobic or even racist, but it is just reality that poor people, black or white, Latino or Asian, are frightening when they are as discouraged and sometimes even strung out as they appear to be at night in downtown LA. In Denver, there are plenty of poor or homeless white people, plenty of scary-looking riffraff who are white; but in LA, the underclass are mostly minorities, which is a source of a lot of racial tension in the city. White people there take it for granted that coming upon a group of rowdy blacks on the street at night is a frightening experience. Were those same whites to live in Denver, they would replace "blacks" with "homeless people", as I think the most scary people at least I see downtown here are discouraged, alcoholic whites.

On this occasion, I had, as I said, only my bus fare; I was walking through the blocks I needed to, to get to my bus stop at Venice Boulevard. On the next corner I could hear some sort of ruckus and yelling, and saw several figures moving around rapidly. I crossed to the other side of the street to pass by this. When I got to that corner, across the street from me 12 or 14 poor blacks were banging on trashcan lids to get attention from cars and passersby. They were selling tee shirts, yelling out deals and prices. Two of them came at me from across the street. I tried to walk as fast as I could, but I know from experience if you ignore people when they speak to you, they take this as a sign that you are afraid, and sometimes will exploit that fear. "Hey!" they yelled at me. "Hey!" "What?" I said. "You want to buy a tee shirt?" "I don't have any money," I said. They seemed satisfied, and left me alone. I was constantly afraid on my way back from work, for the half-hour or so it took to transfer buses downtown.

I would catch my bus at about 6:15 in the morning, on workdays, in order to make it in to work at 9:00. The way back was even slower: by the time I was downtown, the buses were running somewhere between once every 30 minutes to once every hour (or so it seemed at times), and the express buses had stopped running by then. I wouldn't get home on workdays usually until about 10:00 to 10:30 at night, having picked up my dinner at a fast food place on the way. I knew, were I to work full time, it would be impossible to commute to Temple City, where the warehouse was (farther east than East LA), every weekday. I planned on moving out there as soon as I was offered a full-time position. For now, I merely went off to work after getting up around 5:30 a.m., got home late, drank one beer and relaxed for half an hour, and then went to bed. I felt happy enough with this, and I was doing well at my job. But within a month Ibraheem offered me a full-time position, so I prepared myself to move.

98

Once, on my way downtown from Temple City, our bus was passing East LA from just north of it. "Is East LA down that way?" I asked a black man I had been talking to. "Yeah," he said, "why you want to know?" "I've seen movies about East LA," I said, "and I'd like to see it one day." I had been talking to this man, who was obviously poor and drunk, into his middle age and looking worse for the wear, and his friend who was younger and sober. "Why you want to go to East LA?" he said. "Boy, they would eat you up down there." "I would just like to see it," I said. "You and your boys know all about it," he said; "you're a cop: I can tell by that mustache. Not only that, but you're a redneck cop. Your boys know all about East LA." I wore a mustache in those days and had quite a paunch; I knew I didn't look typical LA, but it was a pretty rude awakening to be told I looked like a redneck. "I'm not a cop," I said. "Aren't there any white people in East LA?" "There are," said the drunk man's friend; "but they're all crazy." When the drunk man got off the bus he called out to his friend: "Don't say anything! I can spot a cop, and he's a cop!" I ended up waiting for a bus in East LA a couple weeks later, but the sun was still up; I had been much more afraid in my bus transfers downtown.

Before that man got off the bus I asked him in what neighborhood he lived. "I live in the heart of all this shit!" he said.

99

My announcement that I was moving came at a bad time for Marty. He had epilepsy and had recently been sued for hospital bills after he'd had a seizure that necessitated an ambulance and hospital stay; they were garnishing a good portion of his wages, and just in the past year he'd been given the night shift, which gave him even more stress. A year earlier, someone had come to deliver the legal papers that said he was being sued and must show up in court; I had signed for them, and gave them to him later. "I don't have to worry about that," he said; "all the judge will do is make me pay what I can, and I'm doing that much now." He never showed up to court; now they were taking more out of his wages than he could afford, and I had lent him quite a bit of money already on the rent.

One night, after he knew I was moving, and he was angry over what he viewed as my abandonment of him at the worst possible time (he still hadn't found another place to live), I began to pester him over the $350 or so he owed me on the rent. I didn't want to merely move out, never see him again, and be stuck with a loan that would never be repaid. I was standing right outside the threshold of the open door to his room, and suddenly he yelled at me and picked up a tennis racket. "Get away from here!" he said. He weighed less than 160 pounds and I weighed about 230; I was still fresh from the lessons at the nearby boxing gym I which had only recently quit. I thought that even if he attacked me with the racket, he would end up only receiving a powerful beating; perhaps I was so angry I was only looking for an excuse for this to happen. I pointed my finger at him and said, "You don't threaten me with that!" He walked up to me and slammed his door in my face.

Later that night, I was in my kitchen and he was standing next to the large kitchen table, which was strewn with mail, an open gallon of milk, some dishes and glasses part-full with different juices and drinks.

"You just asked me at the wrong time," he said. "It's always the wrong time with you," I said. He turned the table on its side, spilling its contents all over the floor, and walked back into his room.

100

Just before the summer of 1989, that summer I awakened to my schizophrenia, I was still living with my mother, and got into a verbal fight with my stepfather about the loud music I always played in the shower. I had been about to take a shower, and he had said, "No music." He wouldn't let me bring my boom box into the bathroom. Like any arrogant teenager I engaged him in argument, and ended up making a much bigger issue of it than it had started out as. Finally, angry and stressed, I took a shower without music. My left testicle began to ache in the shower; the ache got progressively worse afterward. An hour after my shower I told my mother about it. I didn't have a doctor at that time, except for my old pediatrician. We got in the car and started driving to his office.

In the car, my testicle ached so badly that every little bump in the road, every little shake of the car, gave me a shot of pain. I was terrified at what was happening to my testicle; I had no idea what could be wrong.

My normal pediatrician wasn't there but there was another doctor who took a look at it. As my scrotum was in his hand, it seemed to shift around on its own, as scrotums sometimes do due to the level of nervousness or comfort, even heat or cold. In any case, while he suggested I go to the hospital, on the way there the pain left me, and I was better.

At the hospital I finally found out what had happened. It was called a tortion, when the testicle gets twisted on whatever it is they hang on, and the blood supply to the testicle is cut off. It had twisted back the right way when the pediatrician looked at it, but there was a danger of it happening again. I was told there was a danger of a second occurrence, unless I got surgery that would secure the testicle from becoming twisted.

This fight with my stepfather was the reason I moved in with my father. It was only one fight in a long series of fights, and one of the worst. My brother and I were talking about this just the other week on the phone. "I moved to Dad's my senior year for the same reason," he told me. "Now I get along with John" (my stepfather) "just fine." "So do I," I said. "I think the problem was with us," said my brother; "I don't think he was really that unreasonable." My brother had moved in with my father before he left for college; now that he was gone it was my turn. I moved into the spare bedroom upstairs in my father's townhouse and waited, somewhat anxiously, for the date of my surgery.

I remember taking acid once in that interval, and thinking to myself, "What if my nut gets twisted again, right now, and I have to go into the hospital for emergency surgery on acid?" It was a terrible thought, but the terrible never came to pass: my surgery went off without a hitch, though there was plenty of pain for about a week afterwards.

A month later, when I was just beginning to lose my mind, Al saw the post-surgical instructions posted on my bedroom door, which my father had placed there and which I hadn't yet taken down. They involved mostly putting ice in the special underwear they gave me for that purpose. "That's some fucked up shit!" said Al. "Damn! You got some fucked up shit to do! That must have been one hell of a surgery. Damn!" He said this as I lay on my bed, stoned, and he was in the hall on his way to the bathroom. I didn't say anything in reply, but let him go on and humiliate me for having to put ice on my testicles, until he was bored with it, and went off to the bathroom where he had been going in the first place.

101

There was a woman, probably in her late 20s, at Ibraheem's factory
that was Mexican by nationality, but had been in the US since she was
a teen, and though she spoke perfect Spanish, she usually preferred to
speak English with me. She spoke that perfectly as well. She had given
up typical Mexican LA style for typical American LA style: she worked
on her body all the time, wore sexy clothes, wore things that especially
flattered her breasts. Her name was Serena. Once, when Ibraheem's
wife Maria and I were standing at one end of the warehouse, Maria
suddenly smelled perfume. "Is that you?" she said. "No," I said. We
both looked to the other end of the warehouse, where Serena had just
opened a door and let a draft blow by her. I smelled the perfume too.
"It's Serena," said Maria. We both laughed.

Serena found me a place to rent, a trailer in the back yard of a 50-
something woman named Lupe, whom she was friends with. It was a
small trailer, the kind you tow behind a truck, maybe 25 feet long,
with running water, a toilet and shower, a propane stove, and a refrig-
erator. I was looking forward to living without roommates, and I
didn't mind a small space.

Ibraheem paid four of his factory workers a little extra to help me
move. I paid for the rental of a Ryder truck, but I didn't have a driver's
license; one of the Mexican factory workers would drive. No small
trucks were available, so I rented a 20-foot truck. Once we were done
loading my things into it, Alexandro, the Mexican who had driven us,
said to me, "All that would have fit in my car." But it's easy enough for
him to say that, I thought, though who would have been blamed if I
had told him it would all fit in his car, and then we got there we found
it didn't? I was anxious to appear on top of things, even with the factory workers.

One of the other Mexicans drove Alexandro's car as Alexandro
drove our truck back to the east side of town. "You know what hap-

pens if that guy gets pulled over in my car?" said Alexandro. "The police take my car. He doesn't have a license. He'll go to jail, and they'll take my car." I think Alexandro had a driver's license himself, but little other documentation; I know he didn't have a Social Security number. But I think I was more worried about it, after he told me this, than he was.

Just when they were dropping me off at my new home, I offered Alexandro $40 for his help. He waved his hand at me, "No, no, I don't need that!" I'm sure he was afraid if Ibraheem found out I had paid him, he would get into trouble since Ibraheem had paid him too. "For your time," I said. "That's worth more than my time," he replied. I put the two 20s back into my wallet, and went to the trailer where I would unpack my things, excited about my new place to live, the new life I was to have here.

There was one thing missing, however. My cat, which I had had for five years, had been out when we went to pick up my things, and I had left him. I would have to go back sometime before the month was up, before my roommates moved out, to pick him up.

I took the bus out there the next weekend, and got a ride back, with my cat in his cramped little carrier, from Angelica, Marty's sister, whom I had rented my first room in LA from, and whom I had remained friends with over the years. We sat and talked in her car as my cat sat in the back. It was night on the way back, and a long drive. We talked about Marty, about how he was doing better now and had found a place to live, and many other things. It was a relaxed night—I felt relaxed with her, as I do with few women. I always felt relaxed with Angelica. Suddenly she said, "How's Isaac" (my cat) "doing?" I looked back at his carrier. He had quit whining and was settled down. "I think he's tired," I said. Suddenly this situation felt charged with meaning for me. Here I was, on a long drive home at night with a woman I was sympathetic with at my side, looking into the back of the car and saying, "He's tired." I hadn't yet given up my dream of one day having a wife and children, which I had wanted at the bottom of my heart for a long time, and here I was with a woman I had at one point fantasized might one day be my wife. For a strange moment, it seemed like we were married, like Isaac wasn't a cat but a little boy sleeping in the back seat, like she wasn't dropping me off but we were driving to a common home after a long day on an outing. The streetlights sent shifting orange beams into the car, on a calm night with little traffic, just as I remembered them doing when I was a child, riding home with my parents in the front seat. It just seemed like this for that moment in which I said, "He's tired," when all of this suddenly appeared clear to me, and then it drifted again out of my consciousness. It made me very happy. I was filled with hope for the future.

102

I remember only two emotions from the time I spent working in Ibraheem's factory fulltime: stress and confusion. The stress was incredible, and the confusion was likewise incredible. I do not really have a sense of how many weeks I worked there fulltime, but it was anywhere between four and eight.

I do not know exactly when the delusion started, when I first got the idea that I was being sucked into working for the Mexican Mafia. I could have had ideas of it before I began fulltime; in any case it didn't turn into a full-blown psychosis until later. I remember realizing that one of Ibraheem's major investors was his father-in-law, a Mexican immigrant who owned a sporting goods store in East LA. Was Ibraheem somehow involved in the Mexican Mafia? Had he married into it? Was he trying to marry me into it? My suspicions weren't exactly dispelled when he said to me one time, giving me a ride somewhere, "I'll find you a wife." He had been going on about all his plans for his business and my part in them; he was a dreamer who hoped to ally me with him in his dreams. Coming from his Lebanese, arranged-marriage culture, he probably assumed he would be doing me every courtesy by finding me a wife. But the effect of his very abstract proposal was to support my ideas that I was working for the Mexican Mafia, and that I could not simply quit my job: I would have to escape.

It was early on that I called in my prescription at a nearby pharmacy, and they told me there was a problem with it. My doctor at that time was on the other side of town, back on the Westside, and I had been seeing him only about once every six months. It sometimes took a few calls from me to his office to get him to refill my prescriptions, but basically I wasn't really seeing him, nor had I been in therapy for years. I didn't bother getting a referral from him to a doctor on my new side of town, or do anything to ensure that I would have medication there. It was something I hadn't even considered.

By the time my doctor finally did refill my prescription, which was before I had completely run out, I had decided that Ibraheem, with his Mafia connections, had decided to interfere with my prescription, and that this was the problem with it. Well, if Ibraheem wanted to see what I would be like without medication, I would show him. Besides, I had bigger things to worry about: I may have to leave the country to escape them, and I couldn't worry about things like medication. I would have to live on my own, without help from medication, if I were to survive in some foreign country as I tried to hide my whereabouts from the Mexican Mafia. First I lowered my dose, then came off all medication completely.

Was Lupe, that woman I rented the trailer from, in on it too? Certainly she was. Someone from work, another Mexican Mafia underling—that Mexican Serena—had found me the place, and was always coming to visit with Lupe. So they had probably set up my trailer beforehand to keep an eye on me, with a phone tap and bugs and hidden cameras. But Serena seemed to know things I had said to people on the bus; she seemed to always be aware of what I had said to anyone, no matter where I was. There must be a bug on my person...but where?...how would they plant one?...my key! The key to the trailer, which I always had in my pocket, was a bug!

This was how I lived for the month or so I worked at Ibraheem's factory, this was what I believed as I struggled to make it to work on time (I was constantly late), write the checks for the bills, call clients about unpaid receivables, answer the phones, handle the shipping, do all the office work I was hired to do. One day, I stepped out of my office, and saw a horrifying, giant red face at the other end of the warehouse, back through the open door and in the room with the sewing machines and their busy operators. I saw this only for a second—I was overwhelmed by it and trying to comprehend what I was seeing—until it turned into the end of a big roll of red clothing material. It had frightened me there for a second—but it was nothing. I was very relieved.

As all this was going on, I was drinking more and more in my off hours. I was too worn out by my job to do the things I needed to for my sustenance—go grocery shopping, cook food—I was hardly eating. I would get home from work, and drink until I could finally forget all this—forget that there were cameras in my trailer looking at me that second, forget that I was bugged. Mostly I wouldn't exactly forget, it would only somehow seem amusing to me. I had a very loud stereo at the time and just enough room to set it up. One night, drinking, I put on some of the more energetic songs from *The Fiddler on the Roof* soundtrack very loud, and began dancing like mad for the pleasure of whoever was watching me though that camera. The camera didn't bother me anymore—it was fun—I was dancing and someone was watching me dance. My movements became wilder and wilder, the trailer shook and shook, until I grew afraid that I would break the flooring, and I stopped. I thought to myself, "Whoever is watching me is very impressed at my dancing—Serena, I think Serena was probably watching me, yes, she was very impressed."

The drinking led me to stay up late at night, and this led me to sleep in and be late for work. One morning I actually tried to do something to let off some of the pressures I was under—I woke up late for work, and called intending to tell them I was quitting. Ibraheem wasn't in, but I spoke to his wife, Maria. "I feel like I'm a liability to the company," I said, "and it would be better if I quit." "We count on you to be here," she said, perhaps a little angrily; "we need you to come in today. If you're going to quit you have to give notice." I got on my bike and rode to work, and on the way I fell off it and gashed my calf on one of the large, front gears. I didn't even know I was bleeding. Right after it happened I immediately began riding again, worried only that I was late for work. I remember someone on the street asking if I was okay. "Yep," I said, ignoring him, and I rode into work.

When I got there, I tried to explain myself, and ended up yelling at Maria, "I've been having a really hard time lately!" Then I went to work on the payables, and noticed I was bleeding at the calf. I went back and asked Maria if she had any rubbing alcohol, and showed her my bloody calf. "You should use peroxide," said Serena, looking at it. "Alcohol will sting." But I told her I preferred rubbing alcohol. I knew I could take a little sting, and I thought somehow it would help me snap out of this distress I was in, like men used to believe a slap or a splash of ice water on the face could cure hysteria. I rubbed my leg with the alcohol and looked at it again. "Do I need stitches?" I asked. "Yes," said Serena; "that's not going to close."

By this time Ibraheem had come in, and I explained I needed stitches. There was a clinic where they took the workers when there was any injury, and Serena offered to drive me. Ibraheem said when I told him I needed stitches, "Let me see it." I showed him, and after hardly a glance he said, "Okay: go get stitches." Serena told me in the car that Ibraheem hated the sight of blood. If a worker were ever injured, he only wanted him or her to go off to the clinic, and didn't generally want to see or inspect the wound at all. The sight of blood was repulsive to him, and he didn't want to deal with it. "I wonder what he thought when his son Omar was born?" said Serena. "That's just life—blood, birth, all that messiness—that's just life." I mentioned to her that I thought it might be because he was a Muslim, as blood is very unclean to Muslims. "But blood and gore is just a part of life—his own child was born bloody, everyone is," she repeated.

At the clinic, though I think most of the doctors and nurses spoke English, Spanish was the first language of most of them, so I used that in talking with them. When they were about to sew up my wound—those two nurses who looked at it, then decided what to do—I said to them, "I don't need anesthesia." "Why do you think not?" said one. "I don't want to pay for it," I said. "But you're under MediCal;" (California's version of Medicaid) "you don't have to worry about paying for it." They ended up giving me local anesthesia. I have no idea why I didn't want it.

When I was out of the clinic, and I saw Serena and Maria there to pick me up (the workday was over by now), I don't know why, but I began to run toward them, like a child running toward some familiar face. Serena called out, "Don't run! Your leg!" I stopped and said to her, "Oh it's fine, it won't break open again."

The next day Ibraheem asked me what had been troubling me so much lately. We were in his car, going back to the clinic, as I had, like a child who feels oversensitive to injuries because of the break he gets from school along with them, become afraid that my leg was getting infected. It wasn't infected at all. I said to Ibraheem when he asked what was troubling me, "I was on a psychological medication for a long time, and since I've moved here I've come off it." He didn't want to hear anything more; I suspect that he didn't want to give me any legal recourse if he decided to fire me later, didn't want me to be able to say it was discrimination. In any case, he didn't want to hear of it.

That night, I found that the delusion had left me. Completely. It had run its course, put me through hell, and then crumbled away. This has happened before in the past. I didn't drink any alcohol that night. I sat out on the grass by my trailer late into the night, calm and at peace, thinking to myself, "I feel so strange—so strange and at peace." I think the strange thing I was feeling was the state of sobriety—I wasn't used to being sober these days. I suppose if our natural consciousness were drunkenness, people might take illegal drugs that put them into a temporary sober state—it would be a powerful addiction, that feeling of clarity, that feeling of comprehension in which the senses are all so acute. I felt at peace finally. But I wasn't thinking clearly enough to go back on my medication; it was only a passing feeling of serenity.

The next morning I woke up early, vomiting. I could not eat any breakfast. I showed up to work on time, but I still felt sick to my stomach. I pulled Ibraheem aside and explained to him that I had quit drinking the night before, and was sick because of it. I didn't eat any lunch because I feared I would throw up, and he let me go early, leaving the UPS shipping to Maria, which was, after all, my job. I didn't really care anymore; I just wanted this job to end doing the least possible harm to Ibraheem's business, lessening as much as possible his financial investment in me. He had been bending over backwards over the past weeks to keep me, even telling me I could show up as late as eleven o'clock if I wanted. He had driven me to the clinic when I didn't need to go; he had given me rides home from work. He wanted to keep me on, and he could tell I was beginning to think this job wasn't working out.

That night I still couldn't hold any food down, and I began to go into a deep, depressed, distressed state of mind. Everything was coming down on me at once—the delusion that had left me, that had been only the last in innumerable anguishing psychoses, my inability to hold a job, the fact that I had moved out here where I knew no one, and no one even knew I was mentally ill. To worsen matters, it was late at night, I couldn't sleep, and I was supposed to show up at work the next day. I had been crying; one of my eyeglass lenses had fallen out of the frame, and I couldn't find the tiny screw to screw it back in. I could not function like this—I could not even see.

I decided what I would do. I put my cat out the door of the trailer, and turned on all the propane on the stove, not lighting any of the burners. Then I lay back on my bed, and waited for death. I waited perhaps five minutes. It was five minutes of terror. I don't know how I can quite describe what it is like to know that, unless you yourself change your mind, you are about to die. It is like being at the very edge of a vast unknown, not understanding abstractly that one day you will go there—but this very minute, in the next fifteen minutes you will be there, and there will be no going back. In perhaps the next ten minutes you will go to sleep—and then whatever happens after death, whether hell, paradise, nothing, or a thousand other possibilities, this will be the irrevocable reality for you. This is why I turned off the propane and aired out my trailer. I was terrified. My pain was agonizing, but at least I could with reasonable certainty know what I would experience in the next fifteen minutes.

I immediately put in an emergency call to my doctor, and explained everything that had happened—my coming off medication, my quitting drinking that made it impossible to hold food down, my suicide "attempt", my recent psychosis, everything. He wanted to admit me to a hospital, and I agreed. I had not been in a hospital for over five years.

103

I was in the hospital for only ten days. Usually, when adult schizophrenics are admitted to hospitals that take state insurance, it is only an emergency measure, and they are discharged as soon as they are relatively stable, even if they don't always have a place to go. As Art, a schizophrenic in his early 30s who had spent his life hitchhiking across the country, told an extremely depressed elderly woman who was always complaining, "You have it good compared to a lot of us. Some of us don't even have a place to go when we are discharged." But I had a place to go; and as soon as I was on medication and had mental health services in my part of town set up for me, I was discharged. I had promised Art I would send a carton of cigarettes up to him as soon as I got out (getting cigarettes was a problem everyone was dealing with at the moment, though most of the patients were generous when they had plenty). I went and bought a carton of Marlboros at a liquor store before taking the bus back to the east side of town, went right back to the security guard on the first floor, and gave him six of the ten packs to send up to Art. When I called Art later that night, I found he had been discharged, but the patient who answered the phone told me, "He was so happy when he got the cigarettes you sent up—he never believed you would do it."

It would be anticlimactic to go through all the things that happened that convinced my parents (whom I had been speaking with daily on the phone after the hospital visit) that I ought to move back to Colorado. There was the deep depression I was in after I was discharged from the hospital and called Ibraheem to tell him finally that I wouldn't be working for him. There was my second, half-hearted suicide attempt, this time with my medication that made me throw up as soon as the bottle of pills hit the back of my throat. There was my second hospital stay after this, which lasted less than three days, this time at a different hospital. There was the fact that I still wasn't eating, though I hadn't been drinking; I simply could not motivate myself to get up and do anything at all.

It was the summer and summers that far from the beach are very hot. The polluted air, which gathers and sits over the San Gabriel Valley, combined with temperatures above a hundred every day, enervate one, and make one feel like one is stuck in some vast, slow wilderness, with no hope of an oasis on the horizon. Perhaps this was only my depression, only me. All I knew was that I woke up at 9:00 in the morning, and my trailer, sitting in the sun, was already unbearably hot. I didn't have anywhere to go to besides my trailer, so I merely sat in it all day, as the heat built and built with the rising of the sun. Sometimes, my stomach would finally motivate me to go and buy a meal, but not every day.

This is how I ended up moving back, finally, to Colorado. When I think of why I moved out to California in the first place, I ask myself, "Why the hell did I stay there six years?" I don't know why to this day. But within a month, I was living in my mother's house, and quite an imposition there; within four months, I was renting a studio apartment in one of the houses my father owns in Denver, and this is the apartment I write to you from.

104

I have been back here in Denver for only a little under two years less than the time I spent in Los Angeles. What has my life been like since then?

I am arguing with my downstairs neighbors about the loud music I am always playing. But soon, they move out; they are replaced by new neighbors, who don't care about the music, and who also move out. The old widow downstairs finally moves in, and she appears to be here to stay. She doesn't mind the music, and finally my stereo quits working and I buy a little boom box radio with a CD player, incapable of playing loud enough to annoy anyone.

I am sitting out on the porch through the long summer days, enjoying the heat now that I have winter to contrast it with. I am enjoying having seasons, enjoying the snow, loving the brief, powerful thunderstorms of summer, looking forward to winter in October, tired of winter and looking forward to summer in April.

I am sitting out on the porch again, waiting for the days to pass by (and the days seem to pass by very quickly), listening to the widow from downstairs go on and on about her past, as her mind jumps from here to there on associations that don't seem obvious to me, but I'm sure are obvious to her. I do not mind listening to her, though she sometimes makes me paranoid, makes me think she has a romantic obsession with me, makes me think it is she who keeps calling me and hanging up when I answer. I get caller ID because of this, and am much more at peace. I sit out and watch the city wind itself up, as the sun climbs higher and higher, then watch the city wind back down, watch the cars become scarce on the streets again for the night. The whole city seems to sleep at night, and in my immediate neighborhood it seems like a city asleep at 1:00 in the morning, not a city whose underside has only now become awake.

I am constantly changing medications for effectiveness and side effects—constantly trying new combinations, trying new drugs, running into problems, becoming suddenly psychotic with one combination, running into bad side effects with another. It is an ongoing process. My doctors are all working on their residencies to become psychiatrists; as soon as one graduates, I am assigned another; but I do not particularly like one over another, just so long as they write my prescriptions. They write down everything I tell them—they have to show this to their supervisors, to get any major changes cleared and checked. There is a very large chart I am building up there, that is handed from one doctor to the next when they change over—a couple pages of handwritten notes are added to it with each of my infrequent sessions. I do not particularly mind this; I am not ashamed of anything I tell them, even if it involves personal things, things like my sexual confusion. I know others will read the notes—but what will they do when they read them?—it will only be very boring reading, and they will forget what they read within an hour.

I am writing, constantly writing. I cannot stop writing. When I was in California and I finished a long project, I seemed to have put everything I had into it, and I would worry that I had absolutely nothing left to say, that I wouldn't be able to write anything else for the rest of my life. I do not worry about that anymore. I finish a novel and two weeks later I have begun the next. I am also submitting my writing. I start to get small pieces published in photocopied, small-circulation zines; this gives me a little thrill and happiness when I receive the free copy in the mail, but little else. The happiness fades a week later.

I get many more rejections than acceptances. I am submitting to book publishers now, big and small, asking them, begging them to just look at a complete manuscript. My only success is Coffee House Press, which requests, over a period of a year and a half, three complete manuscripts, rejecting them all. I sit out even on cold winter days, waiting for the mail to come, hoping for good news. If the mail hasn't come by 2 o'clock and I realize it's a holiday, I feel cheated. I wake up in the morning, drink Turkish coffee, write a few hours, and go down and check the mail. I check the mail again and again before I find it has come.

I am still working on my bachelor's degree, but only very apathetically. I do not care for a bachelor's degree anymore; but my mother pressures me again and again to finish school, and I am only 8, then 7, then 6, then 5 classes away. To appease her, and to keep occupied, I take one class a semester. My parents are happy to pay for it, though if it weren't for my mother I wouldn't care in the least for that piece of paper. Taking classes puts me under stress, since at the University of Colorado at Denver I have the highest GPA of my career: over 3.95. With such a record, I am terrified I will get a B and ruin everything. I like to do well in school; but for some odd reason I would much rather not actually graduate.

I have a bad reaction to a medication, and before I am stabilized I cut my foot on broken glass one night in my sleep. There is a hell of a lot of blood everywhere, and it terrifies me; I don't know where it came from. I call my doctor and tell her I think I may have murdered someone. She calls the police and soon they show up with weapons drawn and pointed at me. But I am very cooperative and sit out on the porch as they search my apartment and take photographs of the blood. They hypothesize that I killed my cat until my cat comes back from his outing in the alleys and streets of my neighborhood. In any case, they find nothing suspicious and take me to the psychological section of the county hospital. I am released the following morning.

I get paranoid thoughts every now and then, but as soon as they threaten to become delusions I call my clinic and talk it over with someone. I take extra medication. I quit drinking for a few months if it has been very bad. I am more and more stable.

Drinking. Islam. I practice Islam for six months or so, only to give it up for good for six months or so, only to fear for the state of my soul and go back to it. I sometimes think if I went to the Catholic church nearby this would be good for me; but Islam has prejudiced me such that I would be betraying my feelings if I went back to worshiping a human being, Jesus. I struggle to pray 5 times a day when practicing Islam; eventually I find nothing better about practicing it, I feel no safer from hell than when I give it up, so that I give it up again. Islam becomes only a meaningless burden when I am fasting and praying. Islam is only a terror to me in the back of my mind when I am not practicing it, the Our'an on my bookshelf a reminder that I am going to hell, that there is so very much about me that is condemnable.

I grow more and more reclusive as the years go by. Christmas, with all the people that come into town, that month of dinners and family get-togethers, is more stressful every year. The more isolated I grow, the harder and more stressful it becomes to interact with people. I sometimes grow lonely, but it is only a passing emotion I am willing to put up with.

I am happy. I would be happy to live like this for the rest of my life. I am happy to write, paint, listen to the radio, smoke my cigarettes, stay locked inside, and live just like I am; I would happily do so forever. I have not realized my dreams. I have become content with what was always within grasp for me, which I either ignored or rejected as an unhappy life. But now I have found it, surrendered to it, and I am happy. I have begun to live that looming "rest of my life" that always troubled me, and made me giddy before a vast unknown, in my youth. I am happy.

105

I sometimes will end a novel with a little story, and I think a little story would be a good ending for this memoir too. Bear with me if I am explaining myself too much; I'm not used to writing autobiography, so I am merely trying to be as honest as possible.

There was once a family who lived in a suburb of Denver, a family of three children, ranging in ages from the little girl at six, to the oldest boy at ten. The parents decided mutually it would be best to divorce, but there was the problem of explaining to the children, especially the young ones, that their father was simply moving out of the house.

They decided they would move to England for a year, and then tell the children they were divorcing. That way it was a neater separation: the father would merely be staying in England, and the children would be the ones moving away—moving back home, that is.

It is the middle child this story deals with. The man that this 8-year-old child was to become would later look back on this year in Yorkshire with several memories. He would remember his friend Philip, remember driving with him to Liverpool or some other beach town, and on the way back Philip would get carsick, and vomit up his dinner. This 8-year-old boy had been driven in a car from Colorado to Illinois without getting carsick before, and he never knew you could get sick from a car—but the sight of Philip's vomit made him vomit just as much. He would remember the swimming lessons he hated, the fact that the teachers in his school took offense if he stuck his hands in his pockets, the little cul-de-sac his house was on, across which Philip's house was on. He would remember that day in school when he dared any other boy to punch him on the shoulder, and they were all amazed, on that concrete schoolyard that looked all the more dreary with the dim English sun, that none of the blows could hurt him at all.

He would remember also someone telling him—he knew it was a woman, but he would have no idea who—that he ought not to ever leave behind the magic every child has within him, within her. This woman would tell him there is a magic about children—a magic in their minds, an innocence or just awe—that allows them to believe anything, to believe in things adults do not have the capacity to consider. Children will believe in wizards and werewolves, this woman said: Don't ever lose that magic you have inside you, don't ever lose your awe and innocence, when you grow up never let die the life of that magical mind.

0-595-23846-7

Made in the USA
Las Vegas, NV
01 October 2021